PENGUIN

Gods and

❖

THE PENGUIN ANTHOLOGY
OF CONTEMPORARY AFRICAN WRITING

ROB SPILLMAN is the editor and cofounder of *Tin House,* a ten-year-old bicoastal literary magazine based in Brooklyn, New York, and Portland, Oregon. *Tin House* has been honored in *The Best American Short Stories, The Best American Essays, The Best American Poetry, The O'Henry Prize Stories,* and *The Pushcart Prize Anthology.* He is also the executive editor of Tin House Books and cofounder of the Tin House Summer Writer's Workshop, now in its seventh year. His articles, book reviews, and essays have appeared in *BookForum, GQ, The New York Times Book Review, Rolling Stone, Spin, Sports Illustrated, Vanity Fair,* and *Vogue,* as well as in many other magazines, newspapers, and anthologies. He lives in Brooklyn, New York.

Gods and Soldiers

THE PENGUIN ANTHOLOGY
OF CONTEMPORARY AFRICAN WRITING

Edited by

· ROB SPILLMAN ·

PENGUIN BOOKS

PENGUIN BOOKS

Published by the Penguin Group
Penguin Group (USA) Inc.,
375 Hudson Street, New York, New York 10014, U.S.A.
Penguin Group (Canada), 90 Eglinton Avenue East, Suite 700, Toronto,
Ontario, Canada M4P 2Y3 (a division of Pearson Penguin Canada Inc.)
Penguin Books Ltd, 80 Strand, London WC2R 0RL, England
Penguin Ireland, 25 St Stephen's Green, Dublin 2,
Ireland (a division of Penguin Books Ltd)
Penguin Group (Australia), 250 Camberwell Road, Camberwell,
Victoria 3124, Australia (a division of Pearson Australia Group Pty Ltd)
Penguin Books India Pvt Ltd, 11 Community Centre,
Panchsheel Park, New Delhi—110 017, India
Penguin Group (NZ), 67 Apollo Drive, Rosedale, North Shore 0623,
New Zealand (a division of Pearson New Zealand Ltd)
Penguin Books (South Africa) (Pty) Ltd, 24 Sturdee Avenue,
Rosebank, Johannesburg 2196, South Africa

Penguin Books Ltd, Registered Offices:
80 Strand, London WC2R 0RL, England

First published in Penguin Books 2009

1 3 5 7 9 10 8 6 4 2

Introduction and selection copyright © Rob Spillman, 2009
All rights reserved

Pages 343–344 constitute an extension of this copyright page.

Publisher's Note
Some of the selections in this book are works of fiction. Names, characters, places, and incidents
either are the product of the author's imagination or are used fictitiously, and any resemblance to actual
persons, living or dead, business establishments, events, or locales is entirely coincidental.

LIBRARY OF CONGRESS CATALOGING-IN-PUBLICATION DATA
Gods and soldiers: the Penguin anthology of current African writing / edited by Rob Spillman.
p. cm.
Includes bibliographical references.
ISBN 978-0-14-311473-4
1. African literature—20th century—Translations into English.   2. African literature (English)—
20th century.   I. Spillman, Rob.
PN849.A352G63 2009
808.8'9960904—dc22   2008038434

Printed in the United States of America
Set in Adobe Garamond • Designed by Elke Sigal
Maps by Deborah Reade

Contents

❖

· Southern Africa ·

Nonfiction

Fiction

Acknowledgments

❖

I would like to thank the many people who offered suggestions and advice, including Pete Ayrton, Elise Cannon, George Makana Clark, Isobel Dixon, Chris Dreyer, Ntone Edjabe, Dedi Felman, Amanda Gersh, D. W. Gibson, Cullen Goldblatt, Neil Gordon, Uzodinma Iweala, Laila Lalami, Johnny Temple, Andy Tepper, Hannah Tinti, Michael Vazquez, Binyavanga Wainaina, and James Woodhouse. I'd also like to thank the invaluable transcription wizardry of Katie Arnold-Ratliff. My wonderfully supportive agent, Betsy Lerner, kept me sane, and Beena Kamlani is the best editor anyone could ever wish for; her boundless enthusiasm, curiosity, and attention to every detail have made this daunting project a pleasure. Lastly, I'd like to thank my wife, Elissa Schappell, and my children, Miles and Isadora, for their continual support.

Introduction

❖

African writing is ready for the international spotlight. Much like the literary scene of India in the late 1980s and early '90s, which spawned the writers Salman Rushdie and Anita Desai, the cultural climate of Africa, with its rapid urbanization coupled with its expanding educational and economic opportunities, has created a hotbed of creativity, heralding the emergence of a vibrant new generation of exciting and innovative writers.

Over the ten years I have been editing the literary journal *Tin House*, I have seen an ever-increasing volume of strong work from African writers, but it wasn't until a few years ago, when I was working on an international issue of *Tin House* magazine, that I threw myself into reading emerging fiction from around the world. During the six months of intense reading leading up to making final selections, I was particularly struck by the work coming out of Africa. There was a palpable sense of urgency in much of the writing. These were stories that had to be written.

More recently, I was a guest editor at a literary festival in Nairobi, a gathering that attracted writers and editors from across Africa. Throughout the week there was a visceral feeling of energy and excitement, like nothing I had experienced before. There was urgency, yes, but also an overall feeling of possibility. The younger writers were mixing forms and languages, appropriating multicultural urban street patois into their stories. From the cradle of civilization, where the world's first stories originated, I was witnessing an African literary renaissance.

Now the rest of the world is tuning in. Young Nigerian Chimamanda Adichie recently won a MacArthur "genius" grant, along with Britain's prestigious Orange Prize and PEN's Beyond Margins Award, and was a finalist for the National Book Critics Circle Award for her novel *Half of a Yellow Sun,* while Chinua Achebe, fifty years after the publication of his groundbreaking novel *Things Fall Apart,* received the Man Booker International Prize for his legendary career. African writers are showing up with regularity in the pages of *The New Yorker* and in American and European literary magazines.

These are the headline grabbers, a mere bucket of sand in the Sahara. From Cairo to Cape Town, new, powerful voices are emerging, and more important, they are finding outlets for their work.

This volume includes a sampling of thirty different authors with a range of publishing experience, from Nobel Prize winners to unknown writers who have yet to publish their first book. The sections are organized geographically, each section opening with a nonfiction selection to provide context. The sections and accompanying maps are included for reference, not to suggest that the selected authors are the only writers to come from any particular region. One could easily create subanthologies featuring hundreds of writers. This anthology is intended as a snapshot of recent writing as seen through the lens of one editor, after consulting with many, many other editors, writers, scholars, critics, and everyday passionate readers.

Some of the themes covered reflect the recent history of the continent: anti-colonialism and the struggle with Western influences, the strongman rule, the rise of women's voices in traditionally patriarchal societies, the personal and national influence of domestic and imported religions—and now, increasingly, what it means to be an independent-minded African in a globalized world.

The nineteenth century saw European nations make huge inroads into the African interior for land, lumber, minerals, and slaves. The old tribal borders gave way to an artificial partitioning of the entire continent by the Europeans in 1885. Belgium had taken over the Congo; France, West Africa, Gabon, and Madagascar; Germany, southwest, east, and central Africa; Britain, with the lion's share, Nigeria, Ghana, and entire swaths of the south, east, and north; Italy, Libya and Somalia; Portugal, Angola and Mozambique; and Spain, an outpost in the western Sahara. African nations only gained independence from their colonizers beginning in the late 1950s, most in the mid-1960s, and inherited the artificial boundaries and groupings left behind by the colonizing powers. An all-too-familiar post-colonial pattern for many countries has been a brief honeymoon followed by dictatorship, either military or strongman rule. Corruption became rampant, and periods of political instability, marked by wars and natural disasters, deepened the plight of the ordinary citizen. Prime examples include ruthless Ugandan strongman Idi Amin; Mobutu Sese Seko, who ruled the Congo with an iron fist for more than thirty years; and Robert Mugabe, Zimbabwe's president since 1980, who is desperately trying to hold on to power despite being voted out in 2008, his country now plunged into economic ruin.

Today, many nations are still struggling to come to grips with postcolonial rule, often teetering between rapid transitions from military to democratic governance, but representative governments are beginning to take hold, however precariously, as witnessed by the surprising violence surrounding the 2007 presidential elections in Kenya, a country generally thought to be the most stable of African countries.

A few key dates to keep in mind:

1841	David Livingstone's first African expedition.
1884–85	The Berlin Conference partitioning Africa among England, France, Germany, Spain, Portugal, Italy, and Belgium.
1956	Britain grants self-rule to Sudan.
1957	The publication of *Things Fall Apart,* by Chinua Achebe; a seminal year for African independence, with Ghana being the first to win independence from Britain.
1960	Cameroon, Senegal, Congo, Ivory Coast, Nigeria, and several other African nations gain independence.
1962	Rwanda, Algeria, and Uganda gain independence.
1963	Kenyan independence.
1967–70	Nigeria-Biafra war.

1975	Angolan independence.
1980	Zimbabwean independence.
1994	South African liberation from apartheid.
1994	Rwandan genocide (an estimated 500,000 to 1 million people killed).
2007	Disputed Kenyan elections.

We open with West Africa, represented here by Ghana, the first black African country to gain independence, and Nigeria, the most populous African country, with 80 million people and, not surprisingly, the richest output of literary work. Nigeria has been plagued by a series of corrupt governments that have exploited the oil-rich nation. Writers have had moments of freedom of expression but also harrowing periods of repression—in 1995, despite an international outcry, the Nigerian military executed the writer Ken Saro-Wiwa-Ogoni for exposing the overly cozy ties and unseemly goings-on between Shell Oil and the military junta.

It has been fifty years since Nigerian Chinua Achebe published his novel *Things Fall Apart,* a classic work of anti-colonialism that became a worldwide literary sensation, its commercial and critical success opening the door for many other black Africans. It seems fitting to reproduce here Achebe's seminal 1965 essay "The African Writer and the English Language," in which he explains why he chooses to write in English versus his native Ibo. Other prominent African writers, most notably Kenyan Ngũgĩ wa Thiong'o, have argued that colonial languages limit African thoughts and ideas, and that Africans should express themselves in their native tongues versus the languages that were imposed upon them. Achebe, on the other hand, makes the case that his African stories and ideas will find a larger audience if written in a more universal language, even within Africa itself, a continent of 800 million people, fifty-four nations, and over two thousand languages.

Art and politics have always been powerful allies in Nigerian fiction. In Helon Habila's masterful story "Lomba," an imprisoned writer is forced to write love poems for the prison superintendent. In Chimamanda Adichie's *Half of a Yellow Sun,* the legacy of the devastating

Biafra-Nigerian civil war is felt on a deeply personal level. Chris Abani and Mohammed Naseehu Ali focus on the changing role of women in traditionally male-dominated societies, Abani portraying the life of a poor prostitute, Ali an empowered Islamic woman whose husband is forced to publicly prove his ability to sexually please his wife.

The next section comprises work from the sub-Saharan former French colonies, commonly referred to as Francophone literature. Francophone culture has been heavily influenced by the concept of Negritude, a movement founded in Paris in the 1930s, which put forth the independence and validity of black culture. This anti-assimilationist philosophy has been closely identified with L. S. Senghor, a Senegalese poet who became the first president of independent Senegal. This black nationalist movement was fueled by the Harlem Renaissance and Haitian artists and championed by French intellectuals like Jean Paul Sartre, who called Negritude "anti-racist racism," and was later embraced by African Americans in the 1960s. Here Cameroonian Patrice Nganang, one of today's most prominent Francophone writers, examines the legacy of Senghor's Negritude and its relevance today.

In an excerpt from her novel *The Belly of the Atlantic,* Fatou Diome shows the long reach of France, via soccer, all the way to a small island off the coast of Senegal, where a boy watches the same game on TV as his sister in France. Alain Mabanckou, with biting humor, renders powerful Congolese thugs hapless through their struggle to master the right phrase of doublespeak, while Boubacar Boris Diop imagines voices for those who were silenced during the brutality of the Rwandan genocide.

While North African writing has similar concerns as that of sub-Saharan Africa, namely, the legacy of colonialism, North African culture has a much longer history of interaction with Europe and the Middle East. In her opening to the North African section, novelist Laila Lalami writes of growing up in a bookish Moroccan household in the 1970s, where, despite the 1956 independence, French children's literature—Alexandre Dumas and Jules Verne—was the main reading in Rabat, and her middle school revelation of discovering native Berber and Arabic authors who were writing of her shared world. When Egyptian feminist Nawal El Saadawi's seminal novel *Woman at Point Zero* appeared in 1974, it stirred controversy for its empathetic portrayal of a high-end prostitute who turns the tables on an abuser. More than thirty years later it still remains a lightning rod for debate about the lives of Arabic women. Mohamed Magani arms himself with humor (and coffee) in an attempt to beat back the repressive French occupation forces in Algeria, while in an excerpt from *The Star of Algiers,* Aziz Chouaki follows the fate of a would-be rocker as he clashes with a fundamentalist movement sweeping his once-tolerant country. In Leila Aboulela's "Souvenirs," a Sudanese man returns to his country after living in Scotland and searches for just the right piece of his homeland to take back to his adopted country.

As we move to East Africa, Binyavanga Wainaina explores the contradictions—modern and ancient, united and fractured—of Kenya, and by extension the rest of Africa. Wainaina, deeply aware of the cliché-ridden lenses through which Westerners perceive his home continent, writes engagingly about stereotypes in his now-legendary tongue-in-cheek essay "How to Write About Africa" for *Granta* in 2005. "Always use the word 'Africa' or 'Darkness' or 'Safari' in your title. . . . Make sure you show how Africans have music and rhythm deep in their souls."

Fellow Kenyan Ngũgĩ wa Thiong'o, in an excerpt from his epic novel *Wizard of the Crow,* wields satire like a scalpel to expose the absurd genuflections of a strongman's sycophants. Abdourahman A. Waberi of Djibouti implodes reality and stereotypes in his surrealistic and comic novel *The United States of Africa,* in which Africa has taken the place of the West as the new beacon of hope and opportunity for the world's immigrants. It is now Africans who look down their noses and prejudge the poor, tired, and huddled masses flocking in from Europe, Asia, and the United States.

In a more realistic vein, the heroine of Somali Nuruddin Farah's novel *Knots,* after a disastrous marriage in Canada, brazenly returns to war-torn Mogadishu to reclaim her familial home from a warlord, while in Ugandan Doreen Baingana's story, a Muslim man converts to Christianity, jettisoning three wives but not his alcoholism or troubles.

❧

Portugal was the last major colonizer to relinquish power in Africa, and only after the fall of the dictator Salazar in 1974. Brutal civil wars in Mozambique and Angola followed, the countries becoming proxy battlegrounds in the Cold War. With recent stability, there has been a greater artistic output from these countries. While popular in Brazil and Portugal, many writers from the former Portuguese colonies are not as frequently translated into English as their French and Arabic-speaking African counterparts. An essay by Mia Couto, the great novelist from Mozambique, eloquently describes how the homogenization of global languages imperils mystery and storytelling. In Angolan Ondjaki's story "Dragonfly," the ineffable beauty of music and everyday objects permeate the conversation between a doctor and a mysterious stranger. In an excerpt from José Eduardo Agualusa's novel *The Book of Chameleons,* Borges is reborn in the form of a chameleon who broodingly passes his days in the library of his master, an albino who invents elaborate family histories for the recently moneyed Angolans, a new class of citizens created in the void left by thirty years of civil war.

The final section of the book is dominated by South Africa. Fifteen years after the end of repressive white minority rule, the entire region is still coping with the aftershocks of apartheid. Nobel laureate J. M. Coetzee has been praised and vilified for his portrayal of conflicted white South Africans, most critics calling his work complex and compelling, while others have accused him of racism. Coetzee himself has said that he considers his sensibilities more aligned with Europe than South Africa, and has recently renounced his citizenship for that of Australia. Here he examines the memoirs of South African poet Breyten Breytenbach, also exiled, then imprisoned for seven years for his anti-apartheid efforts.

The other South African writer to win the Nobel Prize, Nadine Gordimer, is also no stranger to controversy, having recently fallen out with her authorized biographer over the claims of embellishment in some of Gordimer's autobiographical writing. In her story "A Beneficiary," Gordimer, who for over fifty years has chronicled apartheid's effects on all aspects of society, follows a woman going through her mother's apartment after her accidental death, where she peels back the layers on the past and present life of liberal upper-middle-class South Africans.

With the waning of the apartheid era, the new tragedy gripping much of Southern Africa is AIDS. Sadly, many artists and writers have succumbed to the disease, including Zimbabwean writer Yvonne Vera, who died of AIDS in 2005. Vera's short story "Dead Swimmers" captures the fierce bonds between a traditional Shona elder and her modern granddaughter. Grief, in the form of a "professional mourner," takes center stage in the excerpt from Zakes Mda's novel *Ways of Dying*, a comic portrait of the travails of a man hired by rural families to grieve at funerals. Foremost Afrikaans writer Marlene van Niekerk's novel *Agaat* delves into the complex relationship between an aging Afrikaans woman and her black caretaker. Ivan Vladislavić, who is of Croatian descent, overturns the detritus of apartheid in his story "The WHITES ONLY Bench," where curators at an apartheid museum go to great lengths to procure an "authentic" bus bench from the apartheid era. Many younger writers are less concerned with the legacy of apartheid than with the here and now of survival in the new, complex, multicultural reality of South Africa. Niq Mhlongo's unvarnished tales of the new, urban, polyglot life have led some to call him the "voice of the kwaito generation" (*kwaito* being the name of the music that emerged from Johannesburg in the early 1990s, a mix of house and traditional chants). In an excerpt from Mhlongo's novel *Dog Eat Dog*, a black university student tries to outwit a pair of corrupt cops who have caught him drinking in public.

Chinua Achebe, both in *Things Fall Apart* and *Arrow of God*, highlighted the growing tensions between traditional African societies and Western values and norms, which not only challenged but were often opposed to African mores and customs. That dynamic continues still, as revealed in these stories, a dynamic further complicated by the different realities of country and city, of tribal laws and secular governance, of religion and tribe, of the legacy of the past and the promise of the future. This future faces the additional modern problems of AIDS, multinational wars, and, with rapidly spreading Internet access across the continent, greater challenges to tradition and culture.

Nelson Mandela once said that "Africa always brings something new." Now, more than ever, this is true. My hope is that this handful of wonderful writing will open the doorway to a greater exploration of African writing and culture. For links and information about further reading of African literature, you can log on to GodsandSoldiers.com.

—ROB SPILLMAN, *February 2009*

• Africa •

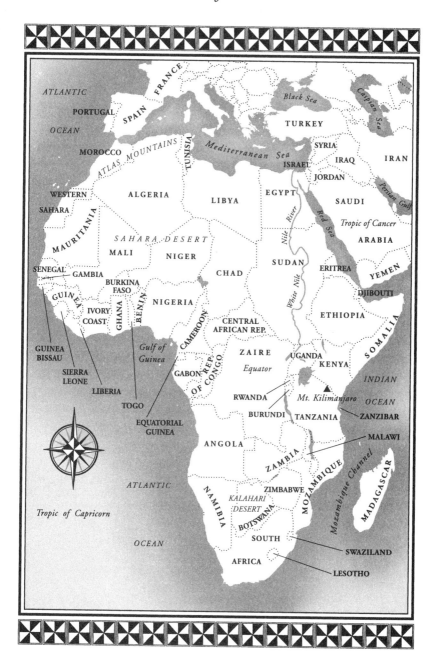

Gods and Soldiers

❖

· West Africa ·

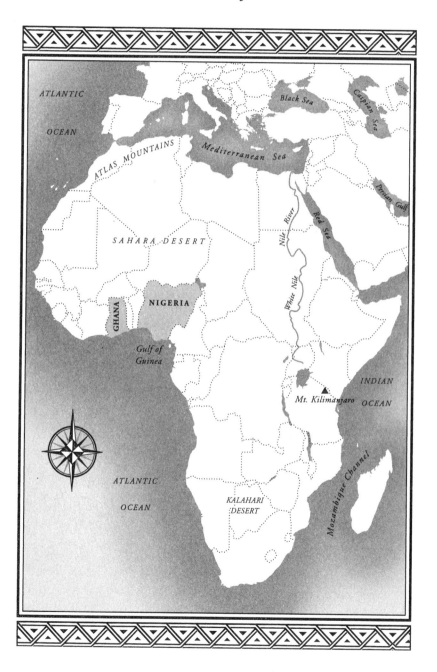

CHINUA ACHEBE

Nigeria

❖

THE AFRICAN WRITER
AND THE ENGLISH LANGUAGE

IN JUNE 1952, there was a writers' gathering at Makerere, impressively styled: "A Conference of African Writers of English Expression." Despite this sonorous and rather solemn title it turned out to be a very lively affair and a very exciting and useful experience for many of us. But there was something which we tried to do and failed—that was to define "African Literature" satisfactorily.

Was it literature produced *in* Africa or *about* Africa? Could African literature be on any subject, or must it have an African theme? Should it embrace the whole continent or South of the Sahara, or just *Black* Africa? And then the question of language. Should it be in indigenous African languages or should it include Arabic, English, French, Portuguese, Afrikaans, etc.?

In the end we gave up trying to find an answer partly—I should admit—on my own instigation. Perhaps we should not have given up so easily. It seems to me from some of the things I have since heard and read that we may have given the impression of not knowing what we were doing, or worse, not daring to look too closely at it.

A Nigerian critic, Obi Wali, writing in *Transition,* volume 10, said: "Perhaps the most important achievement of the conference . . . is that African literature as now defined and understood leads nowhere."

I am sure that Obi Wali must have felt triumphantly vindicated when he saw the report of a different kind of conference held later at Fourah Bay to discuss African literature and the University curriculum.

This conference produced a tentative definition of African literature as follows: "Creative writing in which an African setting is authentically handled or to which experiences originating in Africa are integral." We are told specifically that Conrad's *Heart of Darkness* qualifies as African literature while Graham Greene's *The Heart of the Matter* fails because it could have been set anywhere outside Africa.

A number of interesting speculations issue from this definition, which admittedly is only an interim formulation designed to produce an indisputably desirable end, namely, to introduce African students to literature set in their environment. But I could not help being amused by the curious circumstance in which Conrad, a Pole writing in English, could produce African literature while Peter Abrahams would be ineligible should he write a novel based on his experiences in the West Indies.

What all this suggests to me is that you cannot cram African literature into a small, neat definition. I do not see African literature as one unit but as a group of associated units—in fact the sum total of all the *national* and *ethnic* literatures of Africa.

A national literature is one that takes the whole nation for its province and has a realized or potential audience throughout its territory. In other words, a literature that is written in the *national* language. As ethnic literature is one which is available only to one ethnic group within the nation. If you take Nigeria as an example, the national literature, as I see it, is the literature written in English; and the ethnic literatures are in Hausa, Ibo, Yoruba, Efik, Edo, Ijaw, etc., etc.

Any attempt to define African literature in terms which overlook the complexities of the African scene at the material time is doomed to failure. After the elimination of white rule shall have been completed, the single most important fact in Africa in the second half of the twentieth century will appear to be the rise of the individual nation states. I believe that African literature will follow the same pattern.

What we tend to do today is to think of African literature as a new-born infant. But in fact what we have is a whole generation of new-born infants. Of course, if you only look cursorily one infant is pretty much like another; but in reality each is already set on its own separate journey. Of course, you may group them together on the basis of the language they will speak or the religion of their fathers. Those would all be valid distinctions; but they could not begin to account fully for each individual person carrying, as it were, his own little, unique lodestar of genes.

Those who in talking about African literature want to exclude North Africa because it belongs to a different tradition surely do not suggest that Black Africa is anything like homogenous. What does Shabaan Robert have in common with Christopher Okigbo or Awooner-Williams? Or Mongo Beti of Cameroon and Paris with Nzekwu of Nigeria? What does the champagne-drinking upper-class Creole society described by Easmon of Sierra Leone have in common with the rural folk and fishermen of J. P. Clark's plays? Of course, some of these differences could be accounted for on individual rather than national grounds, but a good deal of it is also environmental.

I have indicated somewhat off-handedly that the national literature of Nigeria and of many other countries of Africa is, or will be, written in English. This may sound like a controversial statement, but it isn't. All I have done has been to look at the reality of present-day Africa. This "reality" may change as a result of deliberate, e.g., political, action. If it does an entirely new situation will arise, and there will be plenty of time to examine it. At present it may be more profitable to look at the scene as it is.

What are the factors which have conspired to place English in the position of national language in many parts of Africa? Quite simply the reason is that these nations were created in the first place by the intervention of the British, which, I hasten to add, is not saying that the peoples comprising these nations were invented by the British.

The country which we know as Nigeria today began not so very long ago as the arbitrary creation of the British. It is true, as William Fagg says in his excellent new book *Nigerian Images,* that this arbitrary action has proved lucky in terms of African art history as an enterprise of the fortunate Princes of Serendip. And I believe that in political and economic terms too this arbitrary creation called Nigeria holds out great prospects. Yet the fact remains that Nigeria was created by the British—for their own ends. Let us give the devil his due: colonialism in Africa disrupted many things, but it did create big political units where there were small, scattered ones before. Nigeria had hundreds of autonomous communities ranging in size from the vast Fulani Empire founded by Usman Dan Dodio in the North to the tiny entities in the East. Today it is one country.

Of course there are areas of Africa where colonialism divided up a single ethnic group among two or even three powers. But on the whole it did bring together many peoples that had hitherto gone their several ways. And it gave them a language with which to talk to one another. If it failed to give them a song, it at least gave them a tongue, for sighing. There are not many countries in Africa today where you could abolish the language of the erstwhile colonial powers and still retain the facility for mutual communication. Therefore those African writers who have chosen to write in English or French are not unpatriotic smart alecs with an eye on the main chance—outside their own countries. They are by-products of the same process that made the new nation-states of Africa.

You can take this argument a stage further to include other countries of Africa. The only reason why we can even talk about African unity is that when we get together we can have a manageable number of languages to talk in—English, French, Arabic.

The other day I had a visit from Joseph Kariuki of Kenya. Although I had read some of his poems and he had read my novels, we had not met before. It didn't seem to matter. In fact, I had met him through his poems, especially through his love poem "Come Away My Love," in which he captures in so few words the trials and tensions of an African in love with a white girl in Britain.

> Come away my love, from streets
> Where unkind eyes divide
> And shop windows reflect our difference.

By contrast, when in 1960 I was traveling in East Africa and went to the home of the late Shabaan Robert, the Swahili poet of Tanganyika, things had been different. We spent some time talking about writing, but there was no real contact. I knew from all accounts that I was talking to an important writer, but of the nature of his work I had no idea. He gave me two books of his poems which I treasure but cannot read—until I have learnt Swahili.

And there are scores of languages I would want to learn if it were possible. Where am I to find the time to learn the half-a-dozen or so Nigerian languages each of which can sustain a literature? I am afraid it cannot be done. These languages will just have to develop as tributaries to feed one central language enjoying nation-wide currency. Today, for good or ill, that language is English. Tomorrow it may be something else, although I very much doubt it.

Those of us who have inherited the English language may not be in a position to appreciate the value of the inheritance. Or we may go on resenting it because it came as part of a package deal which included many other items of doubtful value and the positive atrocity of racial arrogance and prejudice which may yet set the world on fire. But let us not in rejecting the evil throw out the good with it.

Some time last year I was traveling in Brazil, meeting Brazilian writers and artists. A number of the writers I spoke to were concerned about the restriction imposed on them by their use of the Portuguese language. I remember a woman poet saying she had given serious thought to writing in French! And yet their problem is not half as difficult as ours. Portuguese may not have the universal currency of English or French, but at least it is the national language of Brazil with her eighty million or so people, to say nothing of the people of Portugal, Angola, Mozambique, etc.

Of Brazilian authors I have only read, in translation, one novel by Jorge Amado, who is not only Brazil's leading novelist but one of the most important writers in the world. From that one novel, *Gabriella,* I was able to glimpse something of the exciting Afro-Latin culture which is the pride of Brazil and is quite unlike any other culture. Jorge Amado is only one of the many writers Brazil has produced. At their national writers' festival there were literally hundreds of them. But the work of the vast majority will be closed to the rest of the world for ever, including no doubt the work of some excellent writers. There is certainly a great advantage to writing in a world language.

I think I have said enough to give an indication of my thinking on the importance of the world language which history has forced down our throat. Now let us look at some of the most serious handicaps. And let me say straight away that one of the most serious handicaps is *not* the one people talk about most often, namely, that it is impossible for anyone ever to use a second language as effectively as his first. This assertion is compounded of half truth and half bogus mystique. Of course, it is true that the vast majority of people are happier with their first language than with any other. But then the majority of people are not writers. We do have enough examples of writers who have performed the feat of writing effectively in a second language. And I am not thinking of the obvious like Conrad. It would be more germane to our subject to choose African examples.

The first name that comes to my mind is Olaudah Equiano, better known as Gustavus Vass, the African. Equiano was an Ibo, I believe from the village of Iseke in the Orlu division of Eastern Nigeria. He was sold as a slave at a very early age and transported to America. Later he bought his freedom and lived in England. In 1789 he published his life story, a beautifully written document which, among other things, set down for the Europe of his time something of the life and habit of his people in Africa in an attempt to counteract the lies and slander invented by some Europeans to justify the slave trade.

Coming nearer to our times we may recall the attempts in the first quarter of this century by West African nationalists to come together and press for a greater say in the management of their own affairs. One of the most eloquent of that band was the Hon. Casely Hayford of the Gold Coast. His Presidential Address to the National Congress of British West Africa in 1925 was memorable not only for its sound common sense but as a fine example of elegant prose. The governor of Nigeria at the time was compelled to take notice and he did so in characteristic style: he called Hayford's Congress "a self-appointed congregation of educated African gentlemen." We may derive some amusement from the fact that British colonial administrators learnt very little in the following quarter of a century. But at the very least they *did* learn in the end—which is more than one can say for some others.

It is when we come to what is commonly called creative literature that most doubt seems to arise. Obi Wali, whose article "Dead End of African Literature" I referred to, has this to say:

... until these writers and their Western midwives accept the fact that any true African literature must be written in African languages, they would be merely pursuing a dead end, which can only lead to sterility, uncreativity and frustration.

But far from leading to sterility the work of many new African writers is full of the most exciting possibilities.

Take this from Christopher Okigbo's "Limits":

> Suddenly becoming talkative
>   like weaverbird
> Summoned at offside of
>   dream remembered
> Between sleep and waking.
> I hand up my egg-shells
> To you of palm grove,
> Upon whose bamboo towers hang
> Dripping with yesterupwine
> A tiger mask and nude spear. . . .
> Queen of the damp half light,
>   I have had my cleansing.
> Emigrant with air-bourne nose,
>   The he-goat-on-heat.

Or take the poem "Night Rain," in which J. P. Clark captures so well the fear and wonder felt by a child as rain clamours on the thatch-roof at night and his mother, walking about in the dark, moves her simple belongings

> Out of the run of water
> That like ants filing out of the wood
> Will scatter and gain possession
> Of the floor . . .

I think that the picture of water spreading on the floor "like ants filing out of the wood" is beautiful. Of course if you have never made fire with faggots you may miss it. But Clark's inspiration derives from the same source which gave birth to the saying that a man who brings home ant-ridden faggots must be ready for the visit of the lizards.

I do not see any signs of sterility anywhere here. What I do see is a new voice coming out of Africa, speaking of African experience in a world-wide language. So my answer to the question: *Can an African ever learn English well enough to be able to use it effectively in creative writing?* is certainly yes. If on the other hand you ask: *Can he ever learn to use it like a native speaker?* I should say, I hope not. It is neither necessary nor desirable for him to be able to do so. The price a world language must be prepared to pay is submission to many different kinds of use. The African writer should aim to use English in a way that brings out his message best without altering the language to the extent that its value as a medium of international exchange will be lost. He should aim at fashioning out an English which is at once universal and able to carry his peculiar experience. I have in mind here the writer who has something new, something different to say. The nondescript writer has little to tell us, anyway, so he might as well tell it in conventional language and get it over with. If I may use an extravagant simile, he is like a man offering a small, nondescript routine sacrifice for which a chick or less will do. A serious writer must look for an animal whose blood can match the power of his offering.

In this respect Amos Tutuola is a natural. A good instinct has turned his apparent limitation in language into a weapon of great strength— a half-strange dialect that serves him perfectly in the evocation of his bizarre world. His last book, and to my mind, his finest, is proof enough that one can make even an imperfect learnt second language do amazing things. In his book *The Feather Woman of the Jungle* Tutuola's superb story-telling is at last cast in the episodic form which he handles best instead of being painfully stretched on the rack of the novel.

From a natural to a conscious artist: myself, in fact. Allow me to quote a small example, from *Arrow of God*, which may give some idea of how I approach the use of English. The Chief Priest in the story is telling one of his sons why it is necessary to send him to church:

I want one of my sons to join these people and be my eyes there. If there is nothing in it you will come back. But if there is something there you will bring home my share. The world is like a Mask, dancing. If you want to see it well you do not stand in one place. My spirit tells me that those who do not befriend the white man today will be saying *had we known* tomorrow.

Now supposing I had put it another way. Like this, for instance:

I am sending you as my representative among these people— just to be on the safe side in case the new religion develops. One has to move with the times or else one is left behind. I have a hunch that those who fail to come to terms with the white may well regret their lack of foresight.

The material is the same. But the form of the one is *in character* and the other is not. It is largely a matter of instinct, but judgment comes into it too.

You read quite often nowadays of the problems of the African writer having first to think in his mother tongue and then to translate what he has thought into English. If it were such a simple, mechanical process I would agree that it was pointless—the kind of eccentric pursuit you might expect to see in a modern Academy of Lagado: and such a process could not possibly produce some of the exciting poetry and prose which is already appearing.

One final point remains for me to make. The real question is not whether Africans *could* write in English but whether they *ought to*. Is it right that a man should abandon his mother tongue for someone else's. It looks like a dreadful betrayal and produces a guilty feeling.

But for me there is no other choice. I have been given this language and I intend to use it. I hope, though, that there always will be men, like the late Chief Fafunwa, who will choose to write in their native tongue and ensure that our ethnic literature will flourish side-by-side with the national ones. For those of us who opt for English there is much work ahead and much excitement.

Writing in the *London Observer* recently, James Baldwin said:

> My quarrel with English language has been that the language
> reflected none of my experience. But now I began to see the
> matter another way . . . Perhaps the language was not my own
> because I had never attempted to use it, had only learned to
> imitate it. If this were so, then it might be made to bear the
> burden of my experience if I could find the stamina to chal-
> lenge it, and me, to such a test.

I recognize, of course, that Baldwin's problem is not exactly mine, but I
feel that the English language will be able to carry the weight of my
African experience. But it will have to be a new English, still in full
communion with its ancestral home but altered to suit its new African
surroundings.

HELON HABILA

· *Nigeria* ·

✛

LOMBA

IN THE MIDDLE of his second year in prison, Lomba got access to pencil and paper and he started a diary. It was not easy. He had to write in secret, mostly in the early mornings when the night warders, tired of peeping through the door bars, waited impatiently for the morning shift. Most of the entries he simply headed with the days of the week; the exact dates, when he used them, were often incorrect. The first entry was in July 1997, a Friday.

Friday, July 1997
    Today I begin a diary, to say all the things I want to say, to myself, because here in prison there is no one to listen. I express myself. It stops me from standing in the centre of this narrow cell and screaming at the top of my voice. It stops me from jumping up suddenly and bashing my head repeatedly against the wall. Prison chains not so much your hands and feet as it does your voice.
    I express myself. I let my mind soar above these walls to bring back distant, exotic bricks with which I seek to build a more endurable cell within this cell. Prison. Misprison. Dis. Un. Prisoner. See? I write of my state in words of derision, aiming thereby to reduce the weight of these walls on my shoulders, to rediscover my nullified individuality. Here in prison loss of self is often expressed as anger. Anger is the baffled prisoner's attempt to re-crystallize his slowly dissolving self. The anger creeps up on you, like twilight edging out the day. It builds in you silently

until one day it explodes in violence, surprising you. I saw it happen in my first month in prison. A prisoner, without provocation, had attacked an unwary warder at the toilets. The prisoner had come out of a bath-stall and there was the warder before him, monitoring the morning ablutions. Suddenly the prisoner leaped upon him, pulling him by the neck to the ground, grinding him into the black, slimy water that ran in the gutter from the toilets. He pummeled the surprised face repeatedly until other warders came and dragged him away. They beat him to a pulp before throwing him into solitary.

Sometimes the anger leaves you as suddenly as it appeared; then you enter a state of tranquil acceptance. You realize the absolute puerility of your anger: it was nothing but acid, cancer, eating away your bowels in the dark. You accept the inescapability of your fate; and with that, you learn the craft of cunning. You learn ways of surviving—surviving the mindless banality of the walls around you, the incessant harassment from the warders; you learn to hide money in your anus, to hold a cigarette inside your mouth without wetting it. And each day survived is a victory against the jailer, a blow struck for freedom.

My anger lasted a whole year. I remember the exact day it left me. It was a Saturday, the day after a failed escape attempt by two convicted murderers. The warders were more than usually brutal that day; the inmates were on tenterhooks, not knowing from where the next blow would come. We were lined up in rows in our cell, waiting for hours to be addressed by the prison superintendent. When he came his scowl was hard as rock, his eyes were red and singeing, like fire. He paced up and down before us, systematically flagellating us with his harsh, staccato sentences. We listened, our heads bowed, our hearts quaking.

When he left, an inmate, just back from a week in solitary, broke down and began to weep. His hands shook, as if with a life of their own. "What's going to happen next?" he wailed, going from person to person, looking into each face, not waiting for an answer. "We'll be punished. If I go back there I'll die. I can't. I can't." Now he was standing before me, a skinny mass of eczema inflammations, and ringworm, and snot. He couldn't be more than twenty, I thought; what did he do to end up in this dungeon? Then, without thinking, I reached out and patted his shoulder. I even smiled. With a confidence I did not feel I said kindly, "No one will take you back." He collapsed into my arms, soaking my shirt with snot and tears and saliva. "Everything will be all right," I repeated over and over. That was the day the anger left me.

In the over two months that he wrote before he was discovered and his diary seized, Lomba managed to put in quite a large number of entries. Most of them were poems, and letters to various persons from his by now hazy, pre-prison life—letters he can't have meant to send. There were also long soliloquies and desultory interior monologues. The poems were mostly love poems; fugitive lines from poets he had read in school: Donne, Shakespeare, Graves, Eliot, etc. Some were his original compositions rewritten from memory; but a lot were fresh creations— tortured sentimental effusions to women he had known and admired, and perhaps loved. Of course they might have been imaginary beings, fabricated in the smithy of his prison-fevered mind. One of the poems reads like a prayer to a much doubted, but fervently hoped for God:

> Lord, I've had days black as pitch
> And nights crimson as blood,
>
> But they have passed over me, like water.
> Let this one also pass over me, lightly,
> Like a smooth rock rolling down the hill,
> Down my back, my skin, like soothing water.

That, he wrote, was the prayer on his lips the day the cell door opened without warning and the superintendent, flanked by two baton-carrying warders, entered.

Monday, September

I had waited for this; perversely anticipated it with each day that passed, with each surreptitious sentence that I wrote. I knew it was me he came for when he stood there, looking bigger than life, bigger than the low, narrow cell. The two dogs with him licked their chops and growled. Their eyes roved hungrily over the petrified inmates caught sitting, or standing, or crouching; laughing, frowning, scratching—like figures in a movie still.

"Lomba, step forward!" his voice rang out suddenly. In the frozen silence it sounded like glass breaking on concrete, but harsher, without the tinkling. I was on my mattress on the floor, my back propped against the damp wall. I stood up. I stepped forward.

He turned the scowl on me. "So, Lomba. You are."

"Yes. I am Lomba," I said. My voice did not fail me. Then he nodded, almost imperceptibly, to the two warders. They bounded forward eagerly, like game hounds scenting a rabbit. One went to a tiny crevice low in the wall, almost hidden by my mattress. He threw aside the mattress and poked two fingers into the triangular crack. He came out with a thick roll of papers. He looked triumphant as he handed it to the superintendent. Their informer had been exact. The other hound reached unerringly into a tiny hole in the sagging, rain-patterned ceiling and brought out another tube of papers.

"Search. More!" the superintendent barked. He unrolled the tubes. He appeared surprised at the number of sheets in his hands. I was. I didn't know I had written so much. When they were through with the holes and crevices, the dogs turned their noses to my personal effects. They picked up my mattress and shook and sniffed and poked. They ripped off the tattered cloth on its back. There were no papers there. They took the pillow-cum-rucksack (a jeans trouser-leg cut off at mid-thigh and knotted at the ankle) and poured out the contents on to the floor. Two threadbare shirts, one pair of trousers, one plastic comb, one toothbrush, one half-used bar of soap, and a pencil. They swooped on the pencil before it had finished rolling on the floor, almost knocking heads in their haste.

"A pencil!" the superintendent said, shaking his head, exaggerating his amazement. The prisoners were standing in a tight, silent arc. He walked the length of the arc, displaying the papers and pencil, clucking his tongue. "Papers. And pencil. In prison. Can you believe that? In my prison!"

I was sandwiched between the two hounds, watching the drama in silence. I felt removed from it all. Now the superintendent finally turned to me. He bent a little at the waist, pushing his face into mine. I smelt his grating smell; I picked out the white roots beneath his carefully dyed moustache.

"I will ask. Once. Who gave you. Papers?" He spoke like that, in jerky, truncated sentences.

I shook my head. I did my best to meet his red-hot glare. "I don't know."

Some of the inmates gasped, shocked; they mistook my answer for reckless intrepidity. They thought I was foolishly trying to protect my source. But in a few other eyes I saw sympathy. They understood that I had really forgotten where the papers came from.

"Hmm," the superintendent growled. His eyes were on the papers in his hands; he kept folding and unfolding them. I was surprised he had not pounced on me yet. Maybe he was giving me a spell to reconsider my hopeless decision to protect whoever it was I was protecting. The papers. They might have blown in through the door bars on the sentinel wind that sometimes patrolled the prison yard in the evenings. Maybe a sympathetic warder, seeing my yearning for self-expression emblazoned neon-like on my face, had secretly thrust the roll of papers into my hands as he passed me in the yard. Maybe—and this seems more probable—I bought them from another inmate (anything can be bought here in prison, from marijuana to a gun). But I had forgotten. In prison, memory short-circuit is an ally to be cultivated at all costs.

"I repeat. My question. Who gave you the papers?" he thundered into my face, spraying me with spit.

I shook my head. "I have forgotten."

I did not see it, but he must have nodded to one of the hounds. All I felt was the crushing blow on the back of my neck. I pitched forward, stunned by pain and the unexpectedness of it. My face struck the door bars and I fell before the superintendent's boots. I saw blood where my face had touched the floor. I waited. I stared, mesmerized, at the reflection of my eyes in the high gloss of the boots' toecaps. One boot rose and landed on my neck, grinding my face into the floor.

"So. You won't. Talk. You think you are. Tough," he shouted. "You are. Wrong. Twenty years! That is how long I have been dealing with miserable bastards like you. Let this be an example to all of you. Don't. Think you can deceive me. We have our sources of information. You can't. This insect will be taken to solitary and he will be properly dealt with. Until. He is willing to. Talk."

I imagined his eyes rolling balefully round the tight, narrow cell, branding each of the sixty inmates separately. The boot pressed down harder on my neck; I felt a tooth bend at the root.

"Don't think because you are political. Detainees you are untouchable. Wrong. You are all rats. Saboteurs. Anti-government rats. That is all. Rats."

But the superintendent was too well versed in the ways of torture to throw me into solitary that very day. I waited two days before they came and blindfolded me and took me away to the solitary section. In the night. Forty-eight hours. In the first twenty-four hours I waited with my eyes fixed on the door, bracing myself whenever it opened; but it was only the cooks bringing the meal, or the number-check warders come to count the inmates for the night, or the slop-disposal team. In the second twenty-four hours I bowed my head into my chest and refused to look up. I was tired. I refused to eat or speak or move. I was rehearsing for solitary.

They came, at around ten at night. The two hounds. Banging their batons on the door bars, shouting my name, cursing and kicking at anyone in their path. I hastened to my feet before they reached me, my trouser-leg rucksack clutched like a shield in my hands. The light of their torch on my face was like a blow.

"Lomba!"

"Come here! Move!"

"Oya, out. Now!"

I moved, stepping high over the stirring bodies on the floor. The light fell on my rucksack.

"What's that in your hand, eh? Where you think say you dey carry am go? Bring am. Come here! Move!"

Outside. The cell door clanked shut behind us. All the compounds were in darkness. Only security lights from poles shone at the sentry posts. In the distance, the prison wall loomed huge and merciless, like a mountain. Broken bottles. Barbed wire. Then they threw the blindfold over my head. My hands instinctively started to rise, but they were held and forced behind me and cuffed.

"Follow me."

One was before me, the other was behind, prodding me with his baton. I followed the footsteps, stumbling. At first it was easy to say where we were. There were eight compounds within the prison yard; ours was the only one reserved for political detainees. There were four other Awaiting Trial men's compounds surrounding ours. Of the three compounds for convicted criminals, one was for lifers and one, situated far away from the other compounds, was for condemned criminals. Now we had passed the central lawn where the warders conducted their morning parade. We turned left towards the convicted prisoners' compounds, then right towards . . . we turned right again, then straight . . . I followed the boots, now totally disoriented. I realized that the forced march had no purpose to it, or rather its purpose was not to reach anywhere immediately. It was part of the torture. I walked. On and on. I bumped into the front warder whenever he stopped abruptly.

"What? You no de see? Idiot!"

Sometimes I heard their voices exchanging pleasantries and amused chuckles with other warders. We marched for over thirty minutes; my slippered feet were chipped and bloody from hitting into stones. My arms locked behind me robbed me of balance and often I fell down, then I'd be prodded and kicked. At some places—near the light poles— I was able to see brief shimmers of light. At other places the darkness was thick as walls, and eerie. I recalled the shuffling, chain-clanging steps we heard late at nights through our cell window. Reluctant, sad steps. Hanging victims going to the hanging room; or their ghosts returning. We'd lie in the dark, stricken by immobility as the shuffling grew distant and finally faded away.

Now we were on concrete, like a corridor. The steps in front halted. I waited. I heard metal knock against metal, then the creaking of hinges. A hand took my wrist, cold metal touched me as the handcuffs were unlocked. My hands felt light with relief. I must have been standing right before the cell door because when a hand on my back pushed me forward I stumbled inside. I was still blindfolded, but I felt the consistency of the darkness change: it grew thicker, I had to wade through it to feel the walls. That was all: walls so close together that I felt like a man in a hole. I reached down and touched a bunk. I sat down. I heard the door close. I heard footsteps retreating. When I removed the blindfold the darkness remained the same, only now a little air touched my face. I closed my eyes. I don't know how long I remained like that, hunched forward on the bunk, my sore, throbbing feet on the floor, my elbows on my knees, my eyes closed.

As if realizing how close I was to tears, the smells got up from their corners, shook the dust off their buttocks and lined up to make my acquaintance—to distract me from my sad thoughts. I shook their hands one by one. Loneliness Smell, Anger Smell, Waiting Smell, Masturbation Smell, Fear Smell. The most noticeable was Fear Smell; it filled the tiny room from floor to ceiling, edging out the others. I did not cry. I opened my lips and slowly, like a Buddhist chanting his mantra, I prayed:

> Let this one also pass over me, lightly,
> Like a smooth rock rolling down the hill,
> Down my back, my skin, like soothing water.

He was in solitary for three days. This is how he described the cell in his diary: The floor was about six feet by ten, and the ceiling was about seven feet from the floor. There were two pieces of furniture: the iron bunk with its tattered, lice-ridden mat, and the slop bucket in the corner.

His only contact with the outside was when his mess of beans, once daily at six p.m., was pushed into the cell through a tiny flap at the bottom of the wrought-iron door, and at precisely eight p.m. when the cell door was opened for him to take out the slop bucket and replace it with a fresh one. He wrote that the only way he distinguished night from day was by the movement of his bowels—in hunger or in purgation.

Then on the third day, late in the evening, things began to happen. Like Nichodemus, the superintendent came to him, covertly, seeking knowledge.

❖

Third Day, Solitary Cell

When I heard metal touch the lock on the door I sat down from my blind pacing. I composed my countenance. The door opened, bringing in unaccustomed rays of light. I blinked. *"Oh, sweet light, may your face meeting mine bring me good fortune."* When my eyes had adjusted to the light, the superintendent was standing on the threshold—the cell entrance was a tight, brightly lit frame around his looming form. He advanced into the cell and stood in the centre, before me in my disadvantaged position on the bunk. His legs were planted apart, like an A. He looked like a cartoon figure: his jodhpur-like uniform trousers emphasized the skinniness of his calves, where they disappeared into the glass-glossy boots. His stomach bulged and hung like a belted sack. He cleared his voice. When I looked at his face I saw his blubber lips twitching with the effort of an attempted smile. But he couldn't quite carry it off. He started to speak, then stopped abruptly and began to pace the tiny space before the bunk. When he returned to his original position he stopped. Now I noticed the sheaf of papers in his hands. He gestured in my face with it.

"These. Are the. Your papers." His English was more disfigured than usual. He was soaking wet with the effort of saying whatever it was he wanted to say. "I read. All. I read your file again. Also. You are journalist. This is your second year. Here. Awaiting trial. For organizing violence. Demonstration against. Anti-government demonstration against the military legal government." He did not thunder as usual.

"It is not true."

"Eh?" The surprise on his face was comical. "You deny?"

"I did not organize a demonstration. I went there as a reporter."

"Well . . ." He shrugged. "That is not my business. The truth. Will come out at your. Trial."

"But when will that be? I have been forgotten. I am not allowed a lawyer, or visitors. I have been awaiting trial for two years now . . ."

"Do you complain? Look. Twenty years I've worked in prisons all over this country. Nigeria. North. South. East. West. Twenty years. Don't be stupid. Sometimes it is better this way. Can you win a case against government? Wait. Hope."

Now he lowered his voice, like a conspirator. "Maybe there'll be another coup, eh? Maybe the leader will collapse and die. He is mortal, after all. Maybe a civilian government will come. Then. There will be amnesty for all political prisoners. Amnesty. Don't worry. Enjoy yourself."

I looked at him, planted before me like a tree, his hands clasped behind him, the papier-mâché smile on his lips. *Enjoy yourself.* I turned the phrase over and over in my mind. When I lay to sleep rats kept me awake, and mosquitoes, and lice, and hunger, and loneliness. The rats bit at my toes and scuttled around in the low ceiling, sometimes falling on to my face from the holes in the ceiling. *Enjoy yourself.*

"Your papers," he said, thrusting them at me once more. I was not sure if he was offering them to me. "I read them. All. Poems. Letters. Poems, no problem. The letters, illegal. I burned them. Prisoners sometimes smuggle out letters to the press to make us look foolish. Embarrass the government. But the poems are harmless. Love poems. And diaries. You wrote the poems for your girl, isn't it?"

He bent forward, and clapped a hand on my shoulder. I realized with wonder that the man, in his awkward, flatfooted way, was making overtures of friendship to me. My eyes fell on the boot that had stepped on my neck just five days ago. What did he want?

"Perhaps because I work in prison. I wear uniform. You think I don't know poetry, eh? Soyinka, Okigbo, Shakespeare."

It was apparent that he wanted to talk about poems, but he was finding it hard to begin.

"What do you want?" I asked.

He drew back to his full height. "I write poems too. Sometimes," he added quickly when the wonder grew and grew on my face. He dipped his hand into his jacket pocket and came out with a foolscap sheet of paper. He unfolded it and handed it to me. "Read."

It was a poem; handwritten. The title was written in capital letters: "MY LOVE FOR YOU."

Like a man in a dream, I ran my eyes over the bold squiggles. After the first stanza I saw that it was a thinly veiled imitation of one of my poems. I sensed his waiting. He was hardly breathing. I let him wait. Lord, I can't remember another time when I had felt so good. So powerful. I was Samuel Johnson and he was an aspiring poet waiting anxiously for my verdict, asking tremulously, "Sir, is it poetry, is it Pindar?"

I wanted to say, with as much sarcasm as I could put into my voice, "Sir, your poem is both original and interesting, but the part that is interesting is not original, and the part that is original is not interesting." But all I said was, "Not bad, you need to work on it some more."

The eagerness went out of his face and for a fleeting moment the scowl returned. "I promised my lady a poem. She is educated, you know. A teacher. You will write a poem for me. For my lady."

"You want me to write a poem for you?" I tried to mask the surprise, the confusion and, yes, the eagerness in my voice. He was offering me a chance to write.

"I am glad you understand. Her name is Janice. She has been to the university. She has class. Not like other girls. She teaches in my son's school. That is how we met."

Even jailers fall in love, I thought inanely.

"At first she didn't take me seriously. She thought I only wanted to use her and dump her. And. Also. We are of different religion. She is Christian, I am Muslim. But no problem. I love her. But she still doubted. I did not know what to do. Then I saw one of your poems . . . yes, this one." He handed me the poem. "It said everything I wanted to tell her."

It was one of my early poems, rewritten from memory.

"'Three Words.' I gave it to her yesterday when I took her out."

"You gave her my poem?"

"Yes."

"You . . . you told her you wrote it?"

"Yes, yes, of course. I wrote it again in my own hand," he said, unabashed. He had been speaking in a rush; now he drew himself together and, as though to reassert his authority, began to pace the room, speaking in a subdued, measured tone. "I can make life easy for you here. I am the prison superintendent. There is nothing I cannot do, if I want. So write. The poem. For me."

There is nothing I cannot do. You can get me cigarettes, I am sure, and food. You can remove me from solitary. But can you stand me outside these walls, free under the stars? Can you connect the tips of my upraised arms to the stars so that the surge of liberty passes down my body to the soft downy grass beneath my feet?

I asked for paper and pencil. And a book to read.

He was removed from the solitary section that day. The pencil and paper came, the book too. But not the one he had asked for. He wanted Wole Soyinka's prison notes, *The Man Died;* but when it came it was *A Brief History of West Africa.* While writing the poems in the cell, Lomba would sometimes let his mind wander; he'd picture the superintendent and his lady out on a date, how he'd bring out the poem and unfold it and hand it to her and say boldly, "I wrote it for you. Myself."

They sit outside on the verandah at her suggestion. The light from the hanging, wind-swayed Chinese lanterns falls softly on them. The breeze blowing from the lagoon below smells fresh to her nostrils; she loves its dampness on her bare arms and face. She looks at him across the circular table, with its vase holding a single rose. He appears nervous. A thin film of sweat covers his forehead. He removes his cap and dabs at his forehead with a white handkerchief.

"Do you like it, a Chinese restaurant?" he asks, like a father anxious to please his favourite child. It is their first outing together. He pestered her until she gave in. Sometimes she is at a loss what to make of his attentions. She sighs. She turns her plump face to the deep, blue lagoon. A white boat with dark stripes on its sides speeds past; a figure is crouched inside, almost invisible. Her light, flower-patterned gown shivers in the light breeze. She watches him covertly. He handles his chopsticks awkwardly, but determinedly.

"Waiter!" he barks, his mouth full of fish, startling her. "Bring another bottle of wine."

"No. I am all right, really," she says firmly, putting down her chopsticks.

After the meal, which has been quite delicious, he lifts the tiny, wine-filled porcelain cup before him and says: "To you. And me."

She sips her drink, avoiding his eyes.

"I love you, Janice. Very much. I know you think I am not serious. That I only want to suck. The juice and throw away the peel. No." He suddenly dips his hand into the pocket of his well-ironed white kaftan and brings out a yellow paper.

"Read and see." He pushes the paper across the table to her. "I wrote it. For you. A poem."

She opens the paper. It smells faintly of sandalwood. She looks at the title: "Three Words." She reaches past the vase and its single, white rose, past the wine bottle, the wine glasses, and covers his hairy hand with hers briefly. "Thank you."

She reads the poem, shifting in her seat towards the swaying light of the lantern:

Three words

When I hear the waterfall clarity of your laughter
When I see the twilight softness of your eyes

I feel like draping you all over myself, like a cloak,
To be warmed by your warmth.

Your flower-petal innocence, your perennial
Sapling resilience—your endless charms

All these set my mind on wild flights of fancy:
I add word unto word,
I compare adjectives and coin exotic phrases
But they all seem jaded, corny, unworthy
Of saying all I want to say to you.

So I take refuge in these simple words,
Trusting my tone, my hand in yours, when I
Whisper them, to add depth and new
Twists of meaning to them. Three words:
I love you.

With his third or fourth poem for the superintendent, Lomba began to send Janice cryptic messages. She seemed to possess an insatiable appetite for love poems. Every day a warder came to the cell, in the evening, with the same request from the superintendent: "The poem." When he finally ran out of original poems, Lomba began to plagiarize the masters from memory. Here are the opening lines of one:

> Janice, your beauty is to me
> Like those treasures of gold . . .

Another one starts:

> I wonder, my heart, what you and I
> Did till we loved . . .

But it was Lomba's bowdlerization of Sappho's "Ode" that brought the superintendent to the cell door:

> A peer of goddesses she seems to me
> The lady who sits over against me
> Face to face,
> Listening to the sweet tones of my voice,
> And the loveliness of my laughing.
> It is this that sets my heart fluttering
> In my chest,
> For if I gaze on you but for a little while
> I am no longer master of my voice,
> And my tongue lies useless
> And a delicate flame runs over my skin
> No more do I see with my eyes;
> The sweat pours down me
> I am all seized with trembling
> And I grow paler than the grass
> My strength fails me
> And I seem little short of dying.

He came to the cell door less than twenty minutes after the poem had reached him, waving the paper in the air, a real smile splitting his granite face.

"Lomba, come out!" he hollered through the iron bars. Lomba was lying on his wafer-thin mattress, on his back, trying to imagine figures out of the rain designs on the ceiling. The door officer hastily threw open the door.

The superintendent threw a friendly arm over Lomba's shoulders. He was unable to stand still. He walked Lomba up and down the grassy courtyard.

"This poem. Excellent. With this poem. After. I'll ask her for marriage." He was incoherent in his excitement. He raised the paper and read aloud the first line, straining his eyes in the dying light: "'A peer of goddesses she seems to me.' Yes. Excellent. She will be happy. Do you think I should ask her for. Marriage. Today?"

He stood before Lomba, bent forward expectantly, his legs planted in their characteristic A formation.

"Why not?" Lomba answered. A passing warder stared at the superintendent and the prisoner curiously. Twilight fell dully on the broken bottles studded in the concrete of the prison wall.

"Yes. Why not. Good." The superintendent walked up and down, his hands clasped behind him, his head bowed in thought. Finally, he stopped before Lomba and declared gravely: "Tonight. I'll ask her."

Lomba smiled at him, sadly. The superintendent saw the smile; he did not see the sadness.

"Good. You are happy. I am happy too. I'll send you a packet of cigarettes. Two packets. Today. Enjoy. Now go back inside."

He turned abruptly on his heels and marched away.

September

Janice came to see me two days after I wrote her the Sappho. I thought, she has discovered my secret messages, my scriptive Morse tucked innocently in the lines of the poems I've written her.

Two o'clock is compulsory siesta time. The opening of the cell door brought me awake. My limbs felt heavy and lifeless. I feared I might have an infection. The warder came directly to me.

"Oya, get up. The superintendent wan see you." His skin was coarse, coal black. He was fat and his speech came out in laboured gasps. "Oya, get up. Get up," he repeated impatiently.

I was in that lethargic, somnambulistic state condemned people surely fall into when, in total inanition and despair, they await their fate—without fear or hope, because nothing can be changed. No dew-wet finger of light would come poking into the parched gloom of the abyss they tenant. I did not want to write any more poems for the superintendent's lover. I did not want any more of his cigarettes. I was tired of being pointed at behind my back, of being whispered about by the other inmates as the superintendent's informer, his fetch-water. I wanted to recover my lost dignity. Now I realized that I really had no "self" to express; that self had flown away from me the day the chains touched my hands. What is left here is nothing but a mass of protruding bones, unkempt hair and tearful eyes; an asshole for shitting and farting, and a penis that in the mornings grows turgid in vain. This leftover self, this sea-bleached wreck panting on the iron-filing sands of the shores of this penal island is nothing but hot air, and hair, and ears cocked, hopeful . . .

So I said to the warder, "I don't want to see him today. Tell him I'm sick."

The fat face contorted. He raised his baton in Pavlovian response. "What!" But our eyes met. He was smart enough to decipher the bold "No Trespassing" sign written in mine. Smart enough to obey. He moved back, shrugging. "Na you go suffer!" he blustered, and left.

I was aware of the curious eyes staring at me. I closed mine. I willed my mind over the prison walls to other places. Free. I dreamt of standing under the stars, my hands raised, their tips touching the blinking, pulsating electricity of the stars. The rain would be falling. There'd be nothing else: just me and rain and stars and my feet on the wet, downy grass earthing the electricity of freedom.

He returned almost immediately. There was a smirk on his fat face as he handed me a note. I recognized the superintendent's clumsy scrawl. It was brief, a one-liner: *Janice is here. Come. Now.* Truncated, even in writing. I got up and pulled on my sweat-grimed shirt. I slipped my feet into my old, worn-out slippers. I followed the warder. We passed the parade ground, and the convicted men's compound. An iron gate, far to our right, locked permanently, led to the women's wing of the prison. We passed the old laundry, which now served as a barber's shop on Saturdays—the prison's sanitation day. A gun-carrying warder opened a tiny door in the huge gate that led into a foreyard where the prison officials had their offices. I had been here before, once, on my first day in prison. There were cars parked before the offices; cadets in their well-starched uniforms came and went, their young faces looking comically stern. Female secretaries with time on their hands stood in the corridors gossiping. The superintendent's office was not far from the gate; a flight of three concrete steps led up to a thick wooden door, which bore the single word: SUPERINTENDENT.

My guide knocked on it timidly before turning the handle.

"The superintendent wan see am," he informed the secretary. She barely looked up from her typewriter; she nodded. Her eyes were bored, uncurious.

"Enter," the warder said to me, pointing to a curtained doorway beside the secretary's table. I entered. A lady sat in one of the two visitor's armchairs. Back to the door, her elbows rested on the huge Formica-topped table before her. Janice. She was alone. When she turned, I noted that my mental image of her was almost accurate. She was plump. Her face was warm and homely. She came halfway out of her chair, turning it slightly so that it faced the other chair. There was a tentative smile on her face as she asked, "Mr. Lomba?"

I almost said no, surprised by the "Mr." I nodded.

She pointed at the empty chair. "Please sit down." She extended a soft, pudgy hand to me. I took it and marveled at its softness. She was a teacher; the hardness would be in the fingers: the tips of the thumb and middle finger, and the side of the index finger.

"Muftau—the superintendent—will be here soon. He just stepped out," she said. Her voice was clear, a little high-pitched. Her English was correct, each word carefully pronounced and projected. Like in a classroom. I was struck by how clean she looked, squeaky clean; her skin glowed like a child's after a bath. She had obviously taken a lot of trouble with her appearance: her blue evening dress looked almost new, but a slash of red lipstick extended to the left cheek after missing the curve of the lip. She crossed and uncrossed her legs, tapping the left foot on the floor. She was nervous. That was when I realized I had not said a word since I entered.

"Welcome to the prison," I said, unable to think of anything else. She nodded. "Thank you. I told Muftau I wanted to see you. The poems, I just knew it wasn't him writing them. I went along with it for a while, but later I told him."

She opened the tiny handbag in her lap and took out some papers. The poems. She put them on the table and unfolded them, smoothing out the creases, uncurling the edges. "After the Sappho I decided I must see you. It was my favourite poem in school, and I like your version of it."

"Thank you," I said. I liked her directness, her sense of humour.

"So I told him—look, I know who the writer is, he is one of the prisoners, isn't he? That surprised him. He couldn't figure out how I knew. But I was glad he didn't deny it. I told him that. And if we are getting married, there shouldn't be secrets between us, should there?"

Ah, I thought, so my Sappho has worked the magic. Aloud I said, "Congratulations."

She nodded. "Thanks. Muftau is a nice person, really, when you get to know him. His son, Farouk, was in my class—he's finished now—really, you should see them together. So touching. I know he has his awkward side, and that he was once married—but I don't care. After all, I have a little past too. Who doesn't?" she added the last quickly, as if scared she was revealing too much to a stranger. Her left hand went up and down as she spoke, like a hypnotist, like a conductor. After a brief pause, she continued, "After all the pain he's been through with his other wife, he deserves some happiness. She was in the hospital a whole year before she died."

Muftau. The superintendent had a name, and a history, maybe even a soul. I looked at his portrait hanging on the wall. He looked young in it, serious-faced and smart, like the cadet warders outside. I turned to her and said suddenly and sincerely, "I am glad you came. Thanks."

Her face broke into a wide, dimpled smile. She was actually pretty. A little past her prime, past her sell-by date, but still nice, still viable. "Oh, no. I am the one that should be glad. I love meeting poets. I love your poems. Really I do."

"Not all of them are mine."

"I know—but you give them a different feel, a different tone. And also, I discovered your S.O.S. I had to come . . ." She picked the poems off the table and handed them to me. There were thirteen of them. Seven were my originals, six were purloined. She had carefully underlined in red ink certain lines of them—the same line, actually, recurring.

There was a waiting-to-be-congratulated smile on her face as she awaited my comment.

"You noticed," I said.

"Of course I did. S.O.S. It wasn't apparent at first. I began to notice the repetition with the fifth poem. 'Save my soul, a prisoner.'"

"Save my soul, a prisoner" . . . The first time I put down the words, in the third poem, it had been non-deliberate, I was just making alliteration. Then I began to repeat it in the subsequent poems. But how could I tell her that the message wasn't really for her, or for anyone else? It was for myself, perhaps, written by me to my own soul, to every other soul, the collective soul of the universe.

I told her, the first time I wrote it an inmate had died. His name was Thomas. He wasn't sick. He just started vomiting after the afternoon meal, and before the warders came to take him to the clinic, he died. Just like that. He died. Watching his stiffening face, with the mouth open and the eyes staring, as the inmates took him out of the cell, an irrational fear had gripped me. I saw myself being taken out like that, my lifeless arms dangling, brushing the ground. The fear made me sit down, shaking uncontrollably amidst the flurry of movements and voices excited by the tragedy. I was scared. I felt certain I was going to end up like that. Have you ever felt like that, certain that you are going to die? No? I did. I was going to die. My body would end up in some anonymous mortuary, and later in an unmarked grave, and no one would know. No one would care. It happens every day here. I am a political detainee; if I die I am just one antagonist less. That was when I wrote the S.O.S. It was just a message in a bottle, thrown without much hope into the sea . . . I stopped speaking when my hands started to shake. I wanted to put them in my pocket to hide them from her. But she had seen it. She left her seat and came to me. She took both my hands in hers.

· *31* ·

"You'll not die. You'll get out alive. One day it will be all over," she said. Her perfume, mixed with her female smell, rose into my nostrils: flowery, musky. I had forgotten the last time a woman had stood so close to me. Sometimes, in our cell, when the wind blows from the female prison, we'll catch distant sounds of female screams and shouts and even laughter. That is the closest we ever come to women. Only when the wind blows, at the right time, in the right direction. Her hands on mine, her smell, her presence, acted like fire on some huge, prehistoric glacier locked deep in my chest. And when her hand touched my head and the back of my neck, I wept.

When the superintendent returned, my sobbing face was buried in Janice's ample bosom. Her hands were on my head, patting, consoling, like a mother, all the while cooing softly, "One day it will finish."

I pulled away from her. She gave me her handkerchief.

"What is going on? Why is he crying?"

He was standing just within the door—his voice was curious, with a hint of jealousy. I wiped my eyes; I subdued my body's spasms. He advanced slowly into the room and went round to his seat. He remained standing, his hairy hands resting on the table.

"Why is he crying?" he repeated to Janice.

"Because he is a prisoner," Janice replied simply. She was still standing beside me, facing the superintendent.

"Well. So? Is he realizing that just now?"

"Don't be so unkind, Muftau."

I returned the handkerchief to her.

"Muftau, you must help him."

"Help. How?"

"You are the prison superintendent. There's a lot you can do."

"But I can't help him. He is a political detainee. He has not even been tried."

"And you know that he is never going to be tried. He will be kept here for ever, forgotten." Her voice became sharp and indignant. The superintendent drew back his seat and sat down. His eyes were lowered. When he looked up, he said earnestly, "Janice. There's nothing anyone can do for him. I'll be implicating myself. Besides, his lot is far easier than that of the other inmates. I give him things. Cigarettes. Soap. Books. And I let him. Write."

"How can you be so unfeeling! Put yourself in his shoes—two years away from friends, from family, without the power to do anything you wish to do. Two years in CHAINS! How can you talk of cigarettes and soap, as if that were substitute enough for all that he has lost?" She was like a teacher confronting an erring student. Her left hand tapped the table for emphasis as she spoke.

"Well." He looked cowed. His scowl alternated rapidly with a smile. He stared at his portrait on the wall behind her. He spoke in a rush. "Well. I could have done something. Two weeks ago. The Amnesty International. People came. You know, white men. They wanted names of. Political detainees held. Without trial. To pressure the government to release them."

"Well?"

"Well." He still avoided her stare. His eyes touched mine and hastily passed. He picked up a pen and twirled it between his fingers. The pen slipped out of his fingers and fell to the floor. "I didn't. Couldn't. You know . . . I thought he was comfortable. And, he was writing the poems, for you . . ." His voice was almost pleading. Surprisingly, I felt no anger towards him. He was just Man. Man in his basic, rudimentary state, easily moved by powerful emotions like love, lust, anger, greed and fear, but totally dumb to the finer, acquired emotions like pity, mercy, humour and justice.

Janice slowly picked up her bag from the table. There was enormous dignity to her movements. She clasped the bag under her left arm. Her words were slow, almost sad. "I see now that I've made a mistake. You are not really the man I thought you were . . ."

"Janice." He stood up and started coming round to her, but a gesture stopped him.

"No. Let me finish. I want you to contact these people. Give them his name. If you can't do that, then forget you ever knew me."

Her hand brushed my arm as she passed me. He started after her, then stopped halfway across the room. We stared in silence at the curtained doorway, listening to the sound of her heels on the bare floor till it finally died away. He returned slowly to his seat and slumped into it. The wood creaked audibly in the quiet office.

"Go," he said, not looking at me.

The above is the last entry in Lomba's diary. There's no record of how far the superintendent went to help him regain his freedom, but as he told Janice, there was very little to be done for a political detainee—especially since, about a week after that meeting, a coup was attempted against the military leader, General Sani Abacha, by some officers close to him. There was an immediate crackdown on all pro-democracy activists, and the prisons all over the country swelled with political detainees. A lot of those already in detention were transferred randomly to other prisons around the country, for security reasons. Lomba was among them. He was transferred to Agodi Prison in Ibadan. From there he was moved to the far north, to a small desert town called Gashuwa. There is no record of him after that.

A lot of these political prisoners died in detention, although the prominent ones made the headlines—people like Moshood Abiola and General Yar Adua.

But somehow it is hard to imagine that Lomba died. A lot seems to point to the contrary. His diary, his economical expressions show a very sedulous character at work. A survivor. The years in prison must have taught him not to hope too much, not to despair too much—that for the prisoner, nothing kills as surely as too much hope or too much despair. He had learned to survive in tiny atoms, piecemeal, a day at a time. It is probable that in 1998, when the military dictator Abacha died, and his successor, General Abdulsalam Abubakar, dared to open the gates to democracy, and to liberty for the political detainees, Lomba was in the ranks of those released.

This might have been how it happened: Lomba was seated in a dingy cell in Gashuwa, his eyes closed, his mind soaring above the glass-studded prison walls, mingling with the stars and the rain in elemental union of freedom; then the door clanked open, and when he opened his eyes Liberty was standing over him, smiling kindly, extending an arm.

And Liberty said softly, "Come. It is time to go."

And they left, arm in arm.

MOHAMMED NASEEHU ALI

· *Ghana* ·

✦

THE MANHOOD TEST

ON THE DAY of Mr. Rafique's *manhood* test, he woke up at half past three in the morning. He had barely slept, haunted in a dream by images of a market scene, where a group of old women hawked phalluses of every size, shape, and color. He remained lying on the hard-foamed couch in the sitting room, where he had slept for the past week. He pressed his limp penis gently—the way doctors press blood pressure bulbs—hoping it would become fully erect, something he had not seen for three whole weeks.

Mr. Rafique came alert on hearing the loud crows of roosters in the courtyard, and was suddenly overpowered by the crippling fear that had tormented him since the day, about a week ago, when his wife accused him of *unmanliness* at the chief's palace on Zongo Street. To verify the wife's allegations, the chief's *alkali,* or judge, had ordered Mr. Rafique to take the manhood test, a process that required Mr. Rafique to sleep with his wife before an appointed invigilator.

The test was scheduled for half past four this afternoon, and the mere thought of being naked with his wife and in the presence of a third person made Mr. Rafique's body numb. He brushed the fingers of his left hand around the edge of his penis. "Why are you treating me so?" he whispered to himself. "Eh, tell me! Why are you treating me so?" He lifted his head from the pillow to look at his crotch, as though he had expected the penis to answer. "What am I going to do, *yá* Allah!" he said, his voice now just above a whisper. "What am I going to do if I fail?"

Mr. Rafique lifted his arms and silently began to pray in the most distant region of his heart, where no one—not even the two angels said to be guarding each mortal day and night—could hear him. He prayed for a miracle to transform his limp phallus into a bouncing, fully erect one; he begged Allah to steer his destiny clear of the imminent humiliation that threatened to put him and his family to shame.

Mr. Rafique had been married for a little over eight months to a young but worldly woman named Zulaikha. Zulai, as she was called affectionately, was the last of four daughters of Baba Mina, a rich transportation business owner who used to live on Zongo Street. Like other once-very-poor-and-suddenly-turned-rich types, Baba Mina had moved to Nhyiaso, an expensive suburb of Kumasi, as soon as he became wealthy enough. He and his family visited their Zongo Street clan-house only on weekends or whenever there was an important social function.

Zulaikha had been raised a spoiled child. Her parents—her mother especially—never denied her things she desired. She wore expensive blouses and skirts instead of the traditional wrapper and *danchiki* worn by girls her age. And while some of her schoolmates drank water to quench both hunger and thirst during lunch break, Zulai ate boiled eggs and drank Fanta instead. At twelve, she had stood as the tallest girl among her age mates. She was slender, with a curvaceous figure that sent the eyes of men darting wherever she walked. Her thighs were muscular, supported by her long, athletic calves. Zulai also had deep, sensuous lips and eyes that were as clear as the moon at its brightest. Her cheeks were lean and dimpled, her eyebrows dark and silky. Her hair was always "permed," or straightened, its length touching her broad shoulders. By the time she was fourteen, Zulaikha's blouses could no longer contain her large breasts.

Her beauty, coupled with her family's riches, turned her into the most popular and desired teenager among the young men on Zongo Street. Before long, all the rich Muslim men in the city were knocking at her family's door, seeking the young girl's hand in marriage. Her father had planned to marry her off by the time she was sixteen, the usual marriage age for girls; but to the father's shock and disappointment, Zulai one by one rejected the dozen or so suitors he and his clan chose for her. She refused to even see the men when they called, and she even went so far as to threaten killing herself if forced to marry a man she didn't choose herself. Her family then asked her to bring home her own suitor, but she told them point blank that she was not ready to marry until she had finished middle school. Such a thing was unheard of from a girl on Zongo Street.

As all of this unraveled, the street's young men were on a quest to see who would be the first to sleep with Zulaikha. And it wasn't long before one of them succeeded. His name was Muntari, a twenty-one-year-old disco-goer and school dropout who three years later found himself in the middle of a scandal when Zulaikha married his uncle, Mr. Rafique, who lived in the same compound with the young man.

Not long after her first sexual experience, Zulaikha quickly turned into a "sex monster," as some called her. Wild stories about her encounters with men abounded on the street. One was about how she slept with six men, who mounted her one after the other, but she was still left unsatisfied. Another story related how she had sex with a young man until he fainted and fell sick afterwards. Soon Zulaikha's loose sexual behaviour began to drag her clan's name in the mud. Her father then insisted she bring home a suitor, or he would marry her off to the man of his choice. By now most of the men who had earlier sought Zulaikha's hand had left off their pursuit of her, afraid the girl's bad name might tarnish their reputations. A few of them persisted, though, and Mr. Rafique was one of them.

Zulaikha knew from the start that most of the men who sought her hand were rich men with two or three wives already, a practice sanctioned by Islam, the street's predominant religion. The idea of competing for a man's attention with two or three other women, along with its concomitant sexual starvation, seemed repugnant and stifling to Zulai. So, even though Mr. Rafique was only a temporary clerk at a local shea-nut butter co-operative union, he was the one she preferred. She was confident that her father would give him capital to start his own business, or at least offer him a position in his transport company. The truth was, Zulai had a genuine fascination for Mr. Rafique—and because of that not even the knowledge of Mr. Rafique's illegitimate child, Najim, a seven-year-old-boy who lived with his mother on Roman Hill, was enough to change her mind about him. Friends and a few family members tipped Zulai that Najim's mother was a jilted lover, who was still in love with Mr. Rafique and may cause her problems down the line in her marriage. But Zulai merely brushed this aside. Zulai was also captivated by the fact that, unlike all the other suitors, Mr. Rafique was somewhat educated. He had attended school only up to Form Four (the equivalent of twelfth grade), but on a street like Zongo, where most of the folks never stepped foot in an English school classroom, Mr. Rafique and a few others were like one-eyed kings in the kingdom of the blind. But most importantly, Zulai was attracted to Mr. Rafique's handsome appearance. She liked the blazers and suits he wore, even on extremely hot days. In short, he conformed to her ideal of the handsome man: not too tall and not too short either, and definitely without a pot belly, which she abhorred.

Not long after Zulai mentioned Mr. Rafique to her family, rumor reached their ears that he was a drunkard. The family didn't worry too much about the rumor, hoping that, "even if it were true, he will change his ways once he is married and saddled with the responsibility of looking after a family of his own," as Baba Mina said.

At the time of the wedding, Zulaikha was nineteen, three years older than the age at which most girls were married. She was only two years shy of finishing middle school, and some among Baba Mina's clan pleaded that he allow her to finish, but the father said to them, "Of what use would schooling be to a woman? She is going to end up in the kitchen, after all!" With those words, the father sealed off the mouths of those who pleaded with him. Customary rituals were hastily carried out after that, paving the way for the marriage ceremony, which turned out to be one of the grandest functions the city of Kumasi had ever seen. Not that anyone expected less from the bride's wealthy father.

The marriage was on shaky ground from the very beginning. Certain things Zulaikha had not given any thought to before suddenly developed into uncomfortable situations that were rife with the potential of creating serious problems for the marriage. The first involved having to live in the same compound as Muntari, the young man who had deflowered her. Although Muntari's room was located outside the main compound, he went inside at least twice each day to fetch hot bath-water in the mornings and to pick up his supper in the evenings. And as much as Zulai attempted to ignore Muntari's presence in the compound, the two still ran into each other. Now a married woman, Zulai was quite embarrassed about this situation and lived with the constant fear of her pre-marital affair with Muntari being leaked out to her husband.

Zulai's other problem concerned something quite different. Like most buildings on Zongo Street, their house did not have a toilet, which meant that she had to be escorted for about three hundred meters to the public latrine. For Zulaikha, who grew up using a glass toilet in the privacy of her parents' house, to empty one's bowels in the presence of five strangers, all squatting in a row, was not only barbaric and shameful, but depressing. She took care of that problem partly by going to the latrine only at night when the latrine was often empty. She stuck to that schedule, no matter how desperate she was with the need to relieve herself during the day.

However, Zulai's third and last problem was more serious, one that made the first two seem trivial. And here is what created it:

Though Mr. Rafique's womanizing lifestyle prior to his marriage had reached legendary status on Zongo Street, he had somehow failed to keep his erection on the couple's first night together. What occurred was peculiar and shocking to both husband and wife, who had expected nothing short of fireworks on their maiden encounter.

What exactly went wrong that night Mr. Rafique could not understand. When his penis became limp in the middle of intercourse, his first thought was to get up and send a child for a cup of strong coffee from Mallam Sile's tea shop, hoping the hot beverage would re-charge his battery. But Zulaikha, who had heard so much about Mr. Rafique's many affairs with women, was set upon giving him a splendid first night. As he lay pondering she crawled all over him, caressing and kissing his chest and ribs. She grabbed and rubbed Mr. Rafique's penis with her fingers, something he detested when his penis was not erect. He made some gestures to thwart her moves, all the time thinking of the right moment to get up and send for that revivifying cup of coffee. But Zulaikha, who was as aroused as someone on a Malian aphrodisiac, wouldn't let go of him. She became frustrated when she realized her efforts weren't doing any good, and finally blamed it all on herself, that she was too inexperienced for him. But Mr. Rafique was busy entertaining fantasies of the women he had slept with before, hoping he would be aroused by them. This didn't work. Then in a rather annoyed voice he told Zulaikha: "Just lie down and stop moving your hands on me like a snake, you hear?" After that the couple lay awake in awkward silence for the rest of the night. They stared at the ceiling and listened to the sound of their breathing until the rooster's first crow at dawn.

Strangely enough the next morning, Mr. Rafique's penis became as erect as a lamp post on his way to the bath-house. It remained hard for the rest of the day while he was at work. In fact he had to use several creative methods in order to hide the bulge in his trousers. That relieved and reassured him that his inability was caused by anxiety, which he thought he could overcome easily. "I just have to dominate her completely," he said to himself.

On the second night, Mr. Rafique jumped into their bed with a full erection. He was all ready to redeem himself, and to prove to Zulai that he was not an *adaakwa,* a pansy. "I'll show her that I am the man of the two of us," he thought as he pulled the bed-side string to switch off the light. He cautioned himself not to let "her have any control, the way I foolishly allowed her to last night." But no sooner had Mr. Rafique entered his wife when he lost his stiffness again. Suddenly his manhood began to shrink like a popped balloon. Zulai used every trick she knew, but her efforts were futile. Soon, Mr. Rafique's penis became the shadow of a penis, a mere token of his manhood. The same thing happened on the next night and the one that followed.

After the third night's fiasco, Mr. Rafique drank some Alafia Bitters, and Zulaikha too acquired some herbal scents and erotic lavenders, which she hoped would boost their lust and desire for each other; but that too didn't do them any good. What was most upsetting to Mr. Rafique was the fact that, as soon as he prepared to leave home for work in the morning, his penis became erect. He tried to keep his anger and frustration to himself, not quite sure how to share a story like that with anyone. He therefore decided that the only thing that would help him was prayer. And so he prayed.

A month and a half later, the couple's situation remained the same. Mr. Rafique contemplated turning to other women—old girlfriends or the fancy, expensive prostitutes at Hotel de Kingsway, one of the finest in all of Ghana, which he frequented before his marriage—to at least clarify whether his inability occurred only with Zulaikha. But he couldn't bring himself to betray his wife, with whom he was already falling in love, despite their problems.

Eventually Mr. Rafique consoled himself that "Allah is the cause of all things," and that "He alone knows why this is happening." He thought he was either being punished for the promiscuous life he had led during his bachelor days, or Allah was just testing him and waiting for the right time to bless and bring happiness to his marriage, as His Prophet Muhammad promises in the *Hadiths,* or Book of Traditions.

Though Mr. Rafique and his wife were greatly saddened by the turn of events, they recoiled from making it known or seeking help—he because of his male pride and Zulaikha out of fear that more fingers would be pointed at her if news of their problem became known. And so, the couple continued to live in their erotic disenchantment for the next two months, during which a severe tension began to grow between the two. They fought and bickered regularly, often over the most trivial things. For his part, Mr. Rafique had—not without profound sadness— already given up hope that he would be able to lie with his wife. He spent most of his time away from the house, either at work during the day or in front of Rex Cinema in the evening, where he played *da-me,* a complicated version of checkers, with friends until well after midnight. Mr. Rafique's sorrows grew even worse: Zulai acquired the habit of waiting for his arrival each night so she could pick fights with him—fights in which she did nothing but assail his inability.

As time went by, Mr. Rafique assumed the un-Islamic and ungodly act of blaming the "old witches" on the street for his problems. He thought of having a talk with his wife, to tell her "face to face" that her aggressive sex manner was the main cause of his inability. But in the end he feared coming across as a wimp with such an open admission of unmanliness. So he remained silent.

Night after night Mr. Rafique lay awake on his bed, next to his wife, staring into the darkness and contemplating the doom that awaited him the moment Zulaikha opened her mouth to her folks about his

inability. He knew that was bound to happen sooner or later, unless a
dramatic change occurred, which he couldn't fathom.

After three months of bridal incarceration—the period when young
brides were prohibited from leaving the house without an escort, usually a girl or a woman from the man's family—Zulaikha's *veil-lifting*
ceremony took place one Thursday morning. It marked the partial lift-
ing of the ban on her movement, as she was limited to visiting her parents, attend naming ceremonies or funerals, and most importantly, walk
to the public latrine without her usual escorts of young girls. In another
three months, Zulaikha would be permitted to go wherever she wished
to go, as she was naturally expected to be carrying Mr. Rafique's child
by then. This custom—traditional rather than religious, which demanded brides to be virgins—enforced a young bride's loyalty to her
husband during the first six months of marriage.

So far, no one except Mr. Rafique and Zulaikha knew anything
about his inability. She considered revealing the secret to someone in
her clan, but decided against it, afraid that it might be taken as a ploy
for divorce, as used by some women. But Zulai knew she must do something, not only about her husband's inability but her involuntary celi-
bacy. She began to have fantasies of Muntari, and even thought of
seducing him into her bed. The young man obviously didn't want to get
caught in the middle of a marriage scandal; as if he had gotten wind of
Zulaikha's designs, he departed for Agégé, joining the exodus that swept
away Ghana's young men and women to the Nigerian city, in search of
a better life. The couple's problems grew even bigger. They took to
quarreling every night, cursing one another in front of everyone in the
compound.

One evening, Mr. Rafique said good-bye to his wife and left the
house for the cinema-front, to play da-me with friends. He realized on
reaching the game place that he had left behind his pack of cigarettes. He
immediately returned home. But when Mr. Rafique arrived Zulaikha
was not in the house. Zulai, who had gone to the latrine and didn't expect her husband back until much later, had stayed talking to friends
she had met on her way home. Mr. Rafique picked up the pack, but
decided to wait for his wife's return—he had been suspicious of her

comings and goings lately. He paced around the living room, his mind brimming with anger. He glanced at the wall clock at two-minute intervals, growing angrier each time.

Half an hour passed and Zulaikha had not returned. The longer Mr. Rafique waited, the more distrustful and suspicious he became. He stormed out of the room in a great fury and walked across the courtyard to the compound's main entrance. He stood there like a sentry, and lighted one cigarette after the other while he cursed the housefolks, including his mother, Hindu, who had not been able to leave her room for nine years, crippled by a mysterious disease. Mr. Rafique shouted obscenities at the top of his voice, calling the housefolks "hypocrites and traitors."

"If it isn't hypocrisy what is it then, when your own people can't even keep an eye on your woman, eh? Tell me!" he yelled, looking at the children who surrounded him, as if he expected them to console him. "All of them, they are *back-biters;* I know they are waiting to see my downfall. But, she will see when she returns tonight! I'll show her the thing that prevents women from growing beards!" He was screaming and waving his fists at no one in particular.

The housefolks knew better than to say a word to Mr. Rafique. When he was angry he stopped speaking Hausa altogether and shouted at them in English—of which nobody understood even a word—and threatened to bring in his military friends to "discipline everyone." Though Mr. Rafique had never acted on his boast, people were still scared, as the military friends, whose sight alone could send one panicking, visited him dressed in full combat gear, with guns hanging from their shoulders and dynamite dangling from their waistbands. Now, the housefolks didn't say a word when Mr. Rafique ranted and raved about his wife's absence. They merely sat and watched from their verandahs.

About an hour after Mr. Rafique returned home, Zulaikha came trotting into the compound. Mr. Rafique immediately pounced on her, seizing her dress and demanding to know where she had been.

"Let go of me, O! What is all this for," she said, "making a fool out of yourself again, eh?"

"Who are you talking to like that, you bastard-woman! Where've you been? I say, tell me where you have been all this time!"

"Where do you think I went to other than the back-house?" she replied, and gently slapped his hands to free her dress from his grip.

"Look, don't vex me more than you have already!" he shouted, the veins sticking out of his neck. "Was it only the latrine that took you more than one hour? I say, tell me where you have been, before I take action on you!"

"What action are you capable of taking, look at him! I beg, don't scream at me like that! Am I not allowed to talk to my friends on the road when I meet . . ." He didn't let her finish.

"You liar! You pathetic liar! A horrible liar you are! Daughter of liars!" he screamed, waving his index finger in her face.

Much later that night, before the elders, Zulaikha had claimed that it was by mistake, but whether her claim was true or not, she slapped Mr. Rafique's hand as he waved it in her face. He in turn hit her in the face. But, hardly had his hand dropped before she, too, responded with a blow that was three times stronger than his. Mr. Rafique staggered and fell to the ground. The housefolks screamed in shock. What would have ensued would have been disastrous, but one of Mr. Rafique's military friends lived in the next compound; and it was he who overheard the fight and walked over and separated the two. But the couple resumed fighting as soon as they returned to their living room. That night they kept the entire household awake, throwing their furniture around and screaming at each other. They fought until two o'clock in the morning, when the chief's *wazeer,* or delegate, came and separated them. Zulaikha spent what little remained of the night with her in-law, Mr. Rafique's lame mother, while he remained in his room and ranted until the *asubá* worship.

Early the next day, the chief's alkali ordered Zulaikha to return to her family for a three-day *yáji,* or mediation period. One might have expected Zulai to reveal her husband's inability to her family during the yáji, but she did not. However, her folks quickly noticed her flat belly, and without asking her a single question concluded that her barrenness was the reason Zulai and her husband fought so frequently. The family immediately visited a spiritual *mallam,* or medicine man, who proclaimed that Zulai was visited by *men of night,* bad spirits who copulated with married women in their sleep and destroyed their pregnancies.

While Zulaikha was with her family, Mr. Rafique decided it was high time that he, too, see a mallam, for his problem. The medicine man told Mr. Rafique that his inability was a curse, one thrown at him by a rival who had wanted to marry Zulaikha. The mallam never informed him who the mysterious rival was, but he gave Mr. Rafique a talisman and asked him to place it under his mattress before sleeping with his wife the next time. "Wallahi, this is the end of your problem, my son . . . no more sleepy-sleepy manhood," the mallam swore and gazed at the ceiling in supplication to Allah, as he handed Mr. Rafique the tiny red amulet.

On the night Zulaikha returned, Mr. Rafique was confident that the mallam's proclamation would manifest true. But Mr. Rafique once again lost his erection while in action. This particular failure became the straw that broke the "camel's hunched back," as Hamda-Wán, Zongo Street's infamous latrine cleaner, would say when things went awry. The next morning, Mr. Rafique felt he had been conned by the mallam and the spiritual bodies he had invoked for his "miracles." What was worse, Mr. Rafique felt slighted by Allah, to whom he prayed daily to save his marriage. At this point he gave up all hope, and waited for the day when Allah, in His infinite mercy, would make good His promise to help those who cry out to Him in their times of need.

As time went by, Zulai came to accept that nothing could be done to improve her husband's inability. And after a bitter, inner struggle, she decided the only thing that would prevent her name from being dragged into the mud was to disclose his problems to the elders. "The sooner I do this, the better for me," she thought one night. "I must let his people and the streetfolks know that I am not the 'bottomless pit' they think I am . . . my belly can carry a seed, but only if he plants it!"

The following day she went to the chief's palace and lodged a formal complaint with the alkali, charging her husband with *unmanliness*. According to Islamic shari'a law, a wife can seek divorce from her husband on three conditions: (1) If he doesn't provide *chi da sha,* or food and drink for her, (2) If she deems there is no love between her and the husband, and (3) If he is *sick,* or impotent. A husband, on the other hand, is not bound by any strict stipulation and may divorce his wife at will.

Zulai's complaint quickly became news on Zongo Street. Not many believed the wife's accusations, as Najim was clear testimony to Mr. Rafique's manliness. At a hearing in the palace of the Muslim chief on Zongo Street, Mr. Rafique insisted that his manhood was in perfect condition and that his wife's accusation was false, "a mere excuse . . . so that the conniving wench can seek a divorce from me," he said. Zulaikha challenged her husband: "He is not a man, and he knows this himself! Believe me! By Allah, he is not a man!" she swore. The couple began to fight in front of the most revered elders; they screamed and raised fingers in one another's face. The fight was separated, but by the end of the hearing it became impossible even for the wise jurors to decide who was telling the truth. So the alkali decided to give the couple six weeks to either solve their problem or report back to him if they failed to do so.

The weeks that followed were quite brutal for Mr. Rafique. He tried to seal his ears to the countless rumors being spread about him and his marriage. At home, the fights between him and Zulai became regular entertainment for the housefolks, who sat and laughed watching the tragicomedy unfold. Then after an ugly fight that lasted all night, Zulaikha resolved that she would be better off without a husband. The next morning she paid her second visit to the alkali and demanded a divorce from Mr. Rafique on the grounds that he still wasn't a man.

Now, on Zongo Street, divorces of that kind were granted only after the accused husband was proven "unmanly" by a neutral person, usually an old woman appointed by the alkali. The *lafiree,* the name given to the old woman, sat in the same room and observed closely as the husband made love to his wife. She would later report her observations to the alkali, who made the final decision in such cases.

Mr. Rafique's test date was scheduled a week from the day of Zulaikha's divorce petition. It was on a Wednesday, a day generally perceived as ill-omened by the streetfolks—though no one knew exactly why. And since "Days never fail to make their weekly appearance," the test date approached rather too fast for Mr. Rafique, though it seemed to have arrived too slowly for the streetfolks, who were more eager than ever to just see *something* happen to *someone.* Long before it was four-thirty on the appointed day, the palace-front was filled with news and rumor-mongers, who seemed just as apprehensive as the poor husband and wife who now found themselves in a public drama from which they could not escape participating.

About an hour after he woke up on the morning of the test Mr. Rafique was still lying on the couch, his half-erect penis cupped in his left hand. His eyes were dry and itchy from lack of sleep; his mind fatigued by the phalluses he had seen in his nightmares; his body tired from a week of sleeping on the couch. He heard the muezzin's incantations, *"Allahu Akbar, Allahu Akbar,"* God is Great! God is Great!, calling the faithful to worship, the first of their five daily worships to the Creator. He gently rubbed his penis as he listened: *"Assalát hairi minal-naum! Assalát hairi minal-naum!"* Worship is better than sleep! Worship is better than sleep!

The mellifluous, melancholy, yet commanding voice of the crier soothed Mr. Rafique's heart momentarily, ridding him of the thoughts of the impending test. But this didn't last too long, his mind gradually drifting back to his manhood fixation. He sat upright and began to pray: "Let my enemies be disappointed and ashamed of their enmity today, *yá* Allah!" He lifted his arms in the air, with a face full of self-pity. "And to those who doubt my *manliness, yá* Allah," he continued, "prove to them that all power comes from You. Equip me with the strength to perform this test, to which I am maliciously being subjected!"

He closed the prayer by reciting *Áyatul-Kursiyyu,* a verse deemed by most clerics as the second most powerful in the Koran, one that is supposed to work wonders in solving all kinds of problems. Finally, Mr. Rafique raised his arms in the air, spat on his open palms, and rubbed them gently on his face. He murmured, "Ámin," lay back on the couch, and resumed caressing his penis. Before long, Mr. Rafique was once again lost in his activity. But the muezzin's voice, distant and echoing, again reminded Mr. Rafique that it was almost time for worship.

Ash-hadu al-láiláha illallá!, I bear witness there is no God besides Allah!

As if spurred on by the muezzin's cries, Mr. Rafique's penis suddenly began to harden. A minute later, it was as erect and solid as an unripe green plantain—crooked and curved toward his right thigh. Never before in his thirty-eight years had his penis been this hard; it was bewildering. He moved his butt sideways and spread his legs apart, so as to make room for his bulging crotch. Filled with an inner joy, a sudden desire almost drove him to walk into the bedroom and thrust his way into his wife. But a second thought advised him against it. He decided to wait until the test, "before the eyes of that old lafiree and the entire street. Then I will prove to my wife and all my enemies that I am a full-grown man."

Then it dawned on Mr. Rafique that the morning worship was about to begin. In one movement he sprang from the couch and got into his prayer-robe, which concealed the bulge in his loose slacks. He slipped his feet into rubber slippers and sprinted out of the room and into the breezy, dew-scented dawn. Outside, a handful of lazy-boned roosters—that had just awaked—crowed. Mr. Rafique ran all the way to the mosque, reciting *dhikr* under his breath.

Zulaikha was already at the chief's palace when Mr. Rafique arrived at four. She was accompanied by two middle-aged women from her clan, and they sat in the large, high-ceilinged lounge of the palace and waited for Zulai, who was being briefed by the alkali at the time of Mr. Rafique's arrival. Mr. Rafique ignored the women. "Hypocrites," he whispered, stealing a mean glance at the women. "That's what they are, all of them! They act as if they like you, when all they are after is your downfall!" He found an unoccupied bench in the corner and sat to wait for his turn to be briefed by the chief's judge.

The meeting with the alkali lasted no more than five minutes, and as Mr. Rafique walked through the foyer to the test room, he saw at least three dozen faces staring at him through the lounge's many windows. He felt as if the entire city of Kumasi was watching him, eagerly awaiting his downfall. Ever so determined to redeem himself "in the eyes of my enemies," and to "put them all to shame, by Allah," Mr. Rafique ignored the stares and walked confidently into the long, wide corridor that led into the palace's courtyard. He began to think that the presence of the lafiree would actually be to his advantage, because Zulaikha—who would not want to be perceived as a whore by the old woman—would lie still as she received him, in the exact manner expected of a married woman. The test suddenly appeared exciting to Mr. Rafique, who felt blood surging through his half-erect penis as he walked closer to the test room.

After leaving the alkali's office, the old lady and Zulaikha had walked directly to the test room, located at the northern end of the palace compounds. The palace building was composed of three large rectangular houses, each with its own compound and courtyard and rooms numbering up to twenty-four. The test room had only one window that faced the almost-vacant courtyard. The interior of the room was brightly lit by a three-foot fluorescent tube. A double-sized kapok bed was tucked in the left corner of the room and a small table sat beside the bed. The invigilator's chair was placed facing the bed, and in a way that the lafiree would be able to have a clear glimpse of what went on.

Mr. Rafique paused on reaching the door. *"Assalaamu-Alaikum!"* he said and waited for a response. The door was opened by the old woman, who peeked outside. Despite the freckles all over her wrinkled face, the lafiree looked healthy for her age. She was sixty-eight. Her gracious smile, which exposed two gaps in her front teeth, seemed fake to Mr. Rafique, who simply saw her as another of his enemies. Responding to her warm, inviting smile, he grinned maliciously.

"Come inside," the lafiree said, though she was quite aware of Mr. Rafique's animosity. "Call me when you are ready to begin. I will be waiting outside." She smiled as she walked past him.

Mr. Rafique went into the test room.

Meanwhile, a large crowd had gathered outside the chief's palace, to be part of this historical event—for such cases were brought only once in a blue moon to the chief. The older folks on the street claimed that of the few cases that had been brought before to the chief's court, Mr. Rafique's was the only one in which the couple had actually decided to go all the way and perform the test. In earlier cases, many husbands were said to have given their wives a divorce instead of having sex with them in front of a stranger. They stood in small groups, trading rumors about the impending test. A number of women—peanut, yam, and ginger-beer vendors—congregated near the palace gates, and a garrulous woman who claimed to be the best friend of Zulaikha's mother captured their full attention with her story. "The girl's mother did confide in me that the spiritualist they visited told them that the man's *thing* had long been cooked and eaten by witches, at one of their weekly feasts," the woman told her rapt audience. "And would you believe it if I told you that it was no one but his mother who took the *thing* to the feast? Which goes to show that she herself is a witch." The woman lowered her voice. "No wonder she has been lying in a grass bed for nine years! But you didn't hear this from me, O! Okay?" But the rumormonger then went on to describe to the vendors (in full, graphic details) how Mr. Rafique's penis was cut, prepared, and eaten by the witches. The garrulous woman's listeners gasped at every sentence and wondered how she came about the information. But none of them questioned her, afraid they may upset her.

Gathered near the vendors was a group of young men from about the age of sixteen to twenty-three. They, too, speculated about the test. One of them swore that he saw Mr. Rafique as he walked into the palace, and that "his prick looked as if it would tear itself right through his trousers. I tell you, man, that was how hard he was!" the young man said. Then he challenged his listeners to a bet of a hundred cedis each if they doubted his word that Mr. Rafique would pass the test. None of his listeners showed interest in betting, though they all rooted for Mr. Rafique, just as most of the women and girls on the street rooted for Zulaikha.

Zulai's eyes met her husband's as he entered the room. She had not seen him since that morning, when he left for work. She lowered her head and shifted uneasily toward the end of the bed. Mr. Rafique just stood there, not saying a word. Zulai lifted her face, and their eyes met again. He shrugged his shoulders and moved his eyebrows up and down, gesturing—or rather signaling—for them to begin what they had come to do. Zulaikha felt like a whore, a very cheap one for that matter, given that the entire city of Kumasi knew what was about to happen between her and her husband, and the fact that there were people outside the palace waiting for the results made her feel even cheaper. Hatred surged through her, not for Mr. Rafique, but for the streetfolks.

Then things took a rather unexpected, mysterious turn. Zulai bowed her head and suddenly felt a tenderness toward her husband and even blamed herself for all of their marital misfortune. "Our marriage has brought nothing but ruin to him; the disgrace that awaits him once the test is over. I wish I knew what to do to make him do well," she said to herself. "Maybe I should tell the old woman that I was lying about his manhood." But she also knew it was too late for her to alter what everyone on the street already knew—the horses are already lined up before the open field, and the derby cannot be canceled.

For Mr. Rafique's part, looking at his estranged wife suddenly turned him soft, not between his legs, as one might have expected, but in his chest—in his heart. *Why the hurt and the vendetta? Why not forgive everyone, so that you can move on with your life?* Mr. Rafique couldn't believe the thoughts he was having, and was perplexed as well as relieved by these questions.

Zulai, whose head was still bowed, wondered what was going on. She lifted her head to steal a glance at her husband, whose eyes were directed at Zulai. The two were suddenly face to face, eye to eye. And Mr. Rafique saw in his wife's face all the qualities that had drawn him to her some eight months ago: her confidence, charm, and warm personality. As he looked at her large, seductive eyes, he felt an intense passion for her—it was a joyous, yet aching sensation, as he still couldn't rid his mind of the pain of the past months. Mr. Rafique saw himself at an emotional crossroad, not knowing whether to "perform the test or to renounce everything—the test, sex in general, Zulai, the people of Zongo Street, and anything that had been in the way of my happiness." Mr. Rafique, resolved to renounce it all, prepared himself to break the news to his wife and the old woman; he was renouncing the test, and thereby granting Zulai the divorce she had sought.

"By separating myself from the spell sex and love cast on people, I can continue to love her, spiritually, wholly, for the rest of our lives," thought Mr. Rafique. He was just about to speak to Zulai when he heard the lafiree's voice. "Are you two ready?"

"Yes," Mr. Rafique answered calmly.

Zulaikha, utterly confused as to what would happen next, looked away from the door. The lafiree—who had expected to see a lot more than what she saw—seemed disappointed.

"I have changed my mind," said Mr. Rafique, avoiding Zulaikha's eyes.

"What are you talking about?" the old woman cried, grabbing his forearm.

"I don't really know, to tell you the truth, but I won't do it even if you leave the room." He paused, glanced at his wife, and continued. "And I hereby grant her the divorce, one, two, three times!"

"Wait, Rafíku," the old woman said. "Why do you want to do this to yourself? You know what the Zongo people will say, don't you?"

"Yes, I do! But, for all I care, they can say whatever they want to say! My heart tells me I am doing a good thing. That's what matters to me, not what the Zongolese think." The lafiree shuddered at Mr. Rafique's pronouncement. And Zulaikha, who one might have expected to rejoice, sat with eyes half-closed and brows tightly knit, as if she had just received tragic news. Mr. Rafique took a step toward Zulaikha. He lowered his head, and with his left palm on his chest extended his right arm to her, in a gesture of love and respect. *"Ma-assalám,"* he said politely and turned and began to walk out of the room. The women stared at each other and then at his back, still unable to make head or tail of what had taken place.

No sooner had Mr. Rafique walked through the palace gates than rumors started floating around that he had failed the manhood test. By the next day, there were half a dozen new stories, each one a slight variation, salted and spiced as it went from one mouth to the other. Some rumors claimed that Mr. Rafique had actually passed the test, but had soon afterwards pronounced the divorce, as a means of revenge on his wife. One swore that Mr. Rafique's "pen had run out of ink" in the middle of the test. Another maintained that he had failed miserably, that he "wasn't even able to get his *thing* up," to begin with; and that he had never been a *man,* and that Najim was someone else's son after all, a child forced on him by "his harlot-mother" because the real culprit had denied responsibility for the pregnancy.

The lafiree, who had apparently noticed the bulge in Mr. Rafique's trousers when he entered the test room, defended him. She swore by her many years and the *strength* of her dead husband that "the young man Rafíku is a real man! I saw his trouser-front with my two eyes, and believe me I can tell a real *man* when I see one!"

So much for the old woman's attempt to tell the truth of what she saw. The street's rascals nicknamed her "Madam-real-manhood." And to the chagrin of the poor lady, that nickname followed her to her grave.

Life went on as usual on Zongo Street after the dust of this drama settled. Zulaikha's life didn't change much after this event. A rumor soon circulated that she was the one who indeed *killed* Mr. Rafique's penis, as he was virile and had a child before he met her. But Zulai wasn't bothered by these assertions, and continued to live her life in the foolhardy manner she had always lived. She threw away the head scarf worn by married Muslim women and divorcées, exposing her permed hair to the world, and refused to be classified as a *bazawara*, a term that had taken on a derogatory meaning to describe a divorced woman—often seen either as someone with emotional baggage or as damaged goods that men should try to avoid at any cost. She didn't marry again until six years later when she was twenty-five, and it was to a rich man in the capital city, Accra, over two hundred miles away.

Mr. Rafique's life went on too, though in a rather different manner. After he left the palace he had headed straight to Apala Goma, the beer parlour down on Bompata Road. He felt as relieved as a donkey that has returned from a long journey and finally has the load it carried taken off its back. Mr. Rafique felt even more relieved and freer than the donkey, because "the animal never has the choice of carrying or not carrying a load in the first place . . . if it does, it will not carry the load at all. Who likes to suffer? But an ass is an ass, always at the mercy of its master, whereas I am my own master!" As Mr. Rafique contemplated in this manner, he stepped into the doorway of the drinking parlour. "Henceforth, I am going to live my life the way I see fit," he thought while he waited for a double shot of straight gin, the first of many subsequent drinks that night. By the time Mr. Rafique left the bar, around a quarter past midnight, he was as drunk as a pagan celebrating the death of his grandfather. Fortunately for him, the rascals who had the habit of thrashing drunks at night had vacated the street. It surprised Mr. Rafique that as drunk as he was, his thoughts were still clear. He vividly recalled the incidents of the whole day, and grinned to himself.

On reaching the house, Mr. Rafique found the main gate locked from the inside. To avoid trouble between him and Mamman Salisu— Mr. Rafique's self-righteous half brother who denounced his drinking with religious vehemence—Mr. Rafique proceeded further down the compound, to the small concretized prayer lot where the boys and young men in the neighbourhood slept on very hot nights. There was a common saying of the streetfolks: "Men who want to command respect should not sleep in the company of kids." Mr. Rafique laughed and walked to the back of the lot, where straw mats were kept in an old oil drum. He selected a mat and spread it in an empty space between two young men who were both his nephews. After removing his shoes, he curled up on his right side. He closed his eyes and placed his hands between his legs. Mr. Rafique had never before experienced the inner peacefulness he felt at that moment. "They will not get me again! They can drown themselves if they don't like the way I live!" he said to himself at that moment when sleep and consciousness cross paths in their tireless effort to bring Light and Darkness to humanity, to unite Joy with Suffering, to bring Inner Peace to the pulsing heart of Man.

CHRIS ABANI

· *Nigeria* ·

✦

from BECOMING ABIGAIL

AND THIS.

Even this. This memory like all the others was a lie. Like the sound of someone ascending wooden stairs, which she couldn't know because she had never heard it. Still it was as real as this one. A coffin sinking reluctantly into the open mouth of a grave, earth in clods collected around it in a pile like froth from the mouth of a mad dog. And women. Gathered in a cluster of black, like angry crows. Weeping. The sound was something she had heard only in her dreams and in these moments of memory—a keening, loud and sharp, but not brittle like the screeching of glass or the imagined sound of women crying. This was something entirely different. A deep lowing, a presence, dark and palpable, like a shadow emanating from the women, becoming a thing that circled the grave and the mourners in a predatory manner before rising up to the brightness of the sky and the sun, to be replaced by another momentarily.

Always in this memory she stood next to her father, a tall whip of blackness like an undecided but upright cobra. And he held her hand in his, another lie. He was silent, but tears ran down his face. It wasn't the tears that bothered her. It was the way his body shuddered every few moments. Not a sob, it was more like his body was struggling to remember how to breathe, fighting the knowledge that most of him was riding in that coffin sinking into the soft dark loam.

But how could she be sure she remembered this correctly?

He was her father and the coffin held all that was left of her mother, Abigail. This much she was sure of. However, judging by the way everyone spoke of Abigail, there was nothing of her in that dark iroko casket. But how do you remember an event you were not there for? Abigail had died in childbirth and she, Abigail, this Abigail, the daughter not the dead one, the mother, was a baby sleeping in the crook of some aunt's arm completely unaware of the world. She looked up. Her father stood in the doorway to the kitchen and the expression she saw on his face wasn't a lie.

"Dad," she said.

He stood in the doorframe. Light, from the outside security lights and wet from the rain, blew in. He swallowed and collected himself. She was doing the dishes buried up to her elbows in suds.

"Uh, carry on," he said. Turning abruptly, he left.

The first time she saw that expression she'd been eight. He had been drinking, which he did sometimes when he was sad. Although that word, sad, seemed inadequate. And this sadness was the memory of Abigail overwhelming him. When he felt it rise, he would drink and play jazz.

It was late and she should have been in bed. Asleep. But the loud music woke her and drew her out into the living room. It was bright, the light sterile almost, the same fluorescent lighting used in hospitals. The furnishing was sparse. One armchair with wide wooden arms and leather seats and backrest, the leather fading and worn bald in some spots. A couple of beanbags scattered around a fraying rug, and a room divider sloping on one side, broken. Beyond the divider was the dining room. But here, in the living room, under the window that looked out onto a hill and the savanna sloping down it, stood the record player and the stack of records. Her father was in the middle of the room swaying along to "The Girl from Ipanema," clutching a photograph of Abigail to his chest. She walked in and took the photograph from his hands.

"Abigail," he said. Over and over.

"It's all right, Dad, it's just the beer."

"I'm not drunk."

"Then it's the jazz. You know it's not good for you."

But she knew this thing wasn't the jazz, at least not the way he had told her about it on other countless drunken nights. That jazz, she imagined, was something you find down a dark alley taken as a short-cut, and brushing rain from your hair in the dimness of the club found there, you hear the singer crying just for you, while behind her a horn collects all the things she forgot to say, the brushes sweeping it all up against the skin of the drum. This thing with her father, however, was something else, Abigail suspected, something dead and rotting.

"Shhh, go to bed, Dad," she said.

He turned and looked at her and she saw it and recognized what it was. She looked so much like her mother that when he saw her suddenly, she knew he wanted her to be Abigail. Now she realized that there was also something else: a patience, a longing. The way she imagined a devoted bonsai grower stood over a tree.

· *Nigeria* ·

❖

VOICE OF AMERICA

1.

WE WERE SITTING in front of Ambo's provision store drinking the local gin *ogogoro* and Coke and listening to a program called *Music Time in Africa* on the Voice of America. We were mostly young men who were spending our long summer holidays in the village. Some of us whose parents were too poor to pay our school fees spent the period of the long vacation doing odd jobs in the village to enable us to save money to pay our school fees. Someone remarked on how clear the broadcast was, compared to our local radio broadcasts, which were filled with static. The presenter announced that there was a special request from an American girl whose name was Laura Williams for an African song and that she was also interested in pen pals from every part of Africa, especially Nigeria. Onwordi, who had been pensive all this while, rushed to Ambo the shopkeeper, collected a pen and began to take down her address. This immediately led to a scramble among us to get the address, too. We all took it down and folded the piece of paper and put it in our pockets and promised we were going to write as soon as we got home that night.

A debate soon ensued among us concerning the girl who wanted pen pals from Africa.

"Before our letter gets to her, she would have received thousands from the big boys who live in the city of Lagos and would throw our letters into the trash can," Dennis said.

"Yes, you may be right," remarked Sunday, "and besides even if she writes you, both of you may not have anything in common to share. But the boys who live in the city go to night clubs and know the lyrics of the latest songs by Michael Jackson and Dynasty. They are the ones who see the latest movies, not the dead Chinese kung-fu and Sonny Chiba films that Fantasia Cinema screens for us in the village once every month."

"But you can never tell with these Americans, she could be interested in being friends with a real village boy because she lives in the big city herself and is probably tired of city boys." Lucky, who said this, was the oldest among us and had spent three years repeating form four.

"I once met an American lady in Onitsha where I went to buy goods for my shop," Ambo the shopkeeper said. He hardly spoke to us, only listening and smiling and looking at the figures in his *Daily Reckoner* notebook.

We all turned to Ambo in surprise. We knew that he traveled to the famous Onitsha market, which was the biggest market in West Africa, to buy goods every week; we could hardly believe that he had met an American lady. Again, Onitsha market was said to be so big that half of those who came there to buy and sell were not humans but spirits. It was said that a simple way of seeing the spirits when in the market was to bend down and look through your legs at the feet of people walking through. If you looked well and closely enough, you would notice that some of them had feet whose soles did not touch the ground when they walked. These were the spirits. If they got a good bargain from a trader he would discover that the money in his money box miraculously grew every day, but any trader who cheats them would find his money disappearing from his money box without any rational explanation.

"She was wearing an ordinary *Ankara* skirt and blouse made from local fabrics and had come to buy a leather purse and hat from the Hausa traders, she even exchanged a few words in Hausa with the traders. The way she said *ina kwu ana nkwu* was so sweet and melodious it was like listening to a canary singing."

"She was probably a volunteer schoolteacher in one of the girls' secondary schools around Onitsha and has lived here for so long she does not count as an American. We are talking of a real American girl living on American soil." Jekwu, who said this, was Ambo's adversary as a result of a dispute over an old debt and was permanently on the opposite side of any argument with Ambo.

"Well, what I was trying to say was that she may be interested in a village boy. Like the one I saw in Onitsha who was wearing a local dress and spoke Hausa, I am sure she will be interested in a village boy," Ambo said and buried his head in his *Daily Reckoner.*

Someone ordered another round of *ogogoro* and Coke and we all began to drink and became silent as we thought our own thoughts. The moon dipped and everywhere suddenly became dark. One by one we rose and left for our homes.

2.

We were sitting in Ambo's shop one evening when Onwordi swaggered in holding a white envelope with a small American stamp which had an eagle painted on it on its side. He waved it in our faces and was smiling. He called for drinks and we all rushed to him trying to snatch the envelope from his hands.

"She has replied," he said, looking very proud like a man who had unexpectedly caught a big fish with a hook in the small village river. The truth was that we had all forgotten about the announcement on the radio program and I had actually washed the shorts in whose back pocket I had put the paper where I jotted down the address.

Onwordi began to read from the letter to us. The girl's name was Laura Williams. She had recently moved with her parents to a farm in Iowa from a much larger city. She had one more year before finishing high school. She was going to take a class on Africa, Its People and Culture in the fall and was curious to know more about African culture. She wanted to know whether Onwordi lived in the city or in a village. She also wanted to know if he lived close to lots of wild animals like giraffes, lions and chimpanzees. And what kind of food did he generally eat, were they spicy? and how were they prepared? She also wanted to know if he came from a large family. She ended the letter with the phrase *"Yours Laura."*

"Oh my God," Lucky said, "this is a love letter. The American lady is searching for an African husband."

"Eehen, why do you say that?" Onwordi said, clearly very excited about such a prospect. Though he had read the letter over a hundred times and was hoping for such a stroke of good fortune, he had not seen any hint of such in the letter.

"See the way she ended the letter, she was practically telling you that she was yours from now on."

"I think that is the American way of ending letters," Dennis said. He was the most well read amongst us, having read the entire oeuvre of James Hadley Chase and Nick Carter. He used big words and would occasionally refer to some girl in the village as a *doll* and some other as a *dead beat floozy*.

"But that is not even the main issue; she can become your girlfriend in due course if you know how to play your game very well. You could tell her that you have a giraffe farm and that you ride on the back of a tiger to your farm," he continued.

"But she is soon going to ask for your photograph and you know we have no giraffes here and the last we heard of a lion was when one was said to have been sighted by a hunter well over ten years ago," Jekwu said. "You should ask her to send you a ten dollar bill, tell her you want to see what it looks like and when she sends it we can change it in the 'black market' at Onitsha for one thousand naira and use the money for *ogogoro*." Jekwu took a drink and wiped his eyes, which were misting over from the drink.

"If you ask her for money, you are going to scare her away. White women are interested in love and romance. Write her a love letter professing your love for her and asking for her hand in marriage, tell her that you would love to come and join her in America and see what she has to say to that," Dennis said.

"Promise her you'll send her some records by Rex Jim Lawson if she can send you Dynasty's 'Do Me Right,'" Lucky added.

"A guy in my school once had a female pen pal from India, she would ask him to place her letters under his pillow when he slept. At night she would appear in his dreams and make love to him. He said he always woke up in the mornings exhausted and worn out after the marathon lovemaking sessions in the dreams. We do not know how it happened, but he later found out the girl had died years back."

We were all shocked into silence by Dennis's story. Ambo turned up the volume of the radio and we began to listen to the news in special English. The war in Palestine was progressing apace, Blacks in South Africa were still rioting in Soweto and children were dying of hunger in Ethiopia and Eritrea.

Onwordi said nothing. He smiled at our comments, holding the letter close to his chest like somehow hugging a lover. He thanked us for our suggestions and was the first to leave Ambo's shop that night.

3.

Two weeks later, Onwordi walked into the shop again smiling and holding an envelope with an American flag stamp close to his chest once more. We circled him and began to ask him questions. She had written once again. She thanked him for his mail. She was glad to know he lived in a village. She was interested in knowing what life was like in a typical African village. What kind of house did he live in, how did he get his drinking water? What kind of school did he attend and how did he learn to write in English? She said she would love to see his photograph, though she did not have any of hers that she could share with him at the present time. Postal regulations would not permit her to send money by mail but she could take a picture of a ten dollar bill and send it to him if all he really wanted was to see what it looked like. She also said she was interested in knowing about African Talking Drums, did they really talk? She said she looked forward to hearing from him again. We were silent as we listened to him and then we all began to speak at once.

"I was right about her being interested in you; otherwise why would she request for your picture without sending you hers?"

"This shows that women all over the world are coy. She was only being cunning. She really wants to know what you look like before she gets involved with you."

"You should go and borrow a suit from the schoolteacher and go to

Sim Paul's Photo Studio in the morning when he is not yet drunk and let him take a nice shot of you so you can send it to her."

"How about you borrow the schoolteacher's suit and Ambo's shirt and Dennis's black school tie and Lucky's silk flower patterned shirt and Sim Paul's shoes and tell the schoolteacher's wife to lend you her stretching comb to straighten your hair if you can't afford Wellastrech cream; then you'll be like the most handsome suitor in the folktale."

"Who is the most handsome suitor?" Onwordi asked. "I have never heard that folktale." Jekwu cleared his throat and took a sip from his *ogogoro* and Coke and began his story.

"Once in the land of Idu there lived a girl who was the prettiest girl in the entire kingdom. Her beauty shone like the sun and her teeth glittered like pearls whenever she smiled. All the young men in the kingdom asked for her hand in marriage but she turned them down. She turned down the men either because they were too tall or too short or too hairy or not hairy enough. She said since she was the most beautiful girl in the kingdom she could only marry the most handsome man. Her fame soon got to the land of the spirits and the most wicked spirit of them all, Tongo, heard about her and said he was going to marry her. Not only was Tongo the most wicked, he was also the most ugly, possessing only a cracked skull for a head. He was all bones and when he walked his bones rattled. Before setting out to ask for the hand of the maiden in marriage, Tongo went round the land of the spirits to borrow body parts. From the spirit with the straightest pair of legs, he borrowed a straight pair of legs and from the one with the best skin he borrowed a smooth and glowing skin. He went round borrowing body parts until he was transformed into the most handsome man there was. As soon as he walked into Idu on the market day and the maiden set eyes on him, she began following him around until he turned, smiled at her and asked for her hand in marriage. She took him to her parents and hurriedly packed her things, waved them goodbye and followed the handsome suitor.

"On their way to his home, which was across seven rivers and seven hills, she was so busy admiring his handsomeness that she did not grow tired and was not bothered by the fact that they were leaving all the human habitations behind. It was only when they crossed into the land of the spirits and he walked into the first house and came out crooked because he had returned the straight legs to their owner that she began to sense that something was wrong. And so she continued to watch as he returned the skin, the arms, the hair and the other borrowed body parts so that by the time they got to his house, it was only his skull that was left. She wept when she realized she had married an ugly spirit but she knew it was too late to return to the land of the living so she bided her time. When Tongo approached her for lovemaking, she told him to go and borrow all the body parts he had on when he married her. Because Tongo loved her headstrong nature, he agreed. Each time they made love he went round borrowing body parts and when they had a child, the child was a very handsome child and grew into the most handsome man."

We all laughed at the story and advised Onwordi to work at transforming himself into the most handsome man. Ambo advised him to dress in traditional African clothes, that, from what he knew about white people, this was likely to appeal to her more.

"So what are you going to do?" we asked Onwordi, but he only smiled and held his letter tightly as he drank.

The next time *Music Time in Africa* was on the air, we had our pens ready to take down the names of pen pals, but the few that were announced were listeners from other parts of Africa and we all felt disappointed.

We waited for Onwordi to walk in with a letter but he did not for quite some time. We wondered what had happened. When he finally walked in after some days, he looked dejected and would not say a word to any of us.

"Hope you have not upset her with your last mail?" Lucky said. "You know white people are very sensitive and you may have hurt her feelings without knowing it."

"This is why we told you to always let us see the letter before you send it to her; when we put our heads together and craft a letter to her, she will pack her things and move into your house, leaking roof and all. As the elders say, 'When you piss on one spot, it is more likely to froth.'"

"But exactly what did you write to her that has made her silent?"

Lucky asked. Onwordi was silent but he smiled liked a dumb man that had accidentally glimpsed a young woman's pointed breast and ordered more drinks. "Or have you started hiding her mail from us? Maybe the contents are too intimate for our eyes. Or now that you have become closer has she started kissing her letters with lipstick-painted lips and sealing the letters with kisses?" Ambo teased. But nothing we said would make Onwordi say a word.

Onwordi walked into Ambo's shop after a period of three weeks holding the envelope that we had become used to by now and looking morose. We all turned to him and began to speak at once.

"What happened, has she confessed that she has a husband or why are you looking so sad?"

"Has she fallen in love with another man? I hear white women fall out of love as quickly as they fall in love."

"If you have her telephone number I can take you to the Post and Telegrams Office in Onitsha if you have the money and help you make a call to her," Ambo suggested.

Onwordi opened the envelope and brought out a photograph. We all crowded around him to take a closer look. It was the picture of the American girl Laura Williams. It was a portrait that showed only her face. She had an open friendly face with brown hair and slightly chubby cheeks. She was smiling brightly in the photograph. Our damp fingers were already leaving a smudge on the face.

"She is beautiful and looks really friendly but why did she not send you a photograph where her legs are showing? That way you do not end up marrying a cripple."

Onwordi was not smiling.

"So what did she say in her letter or have the contents become too intimate for you to share with us?"

"She says that this was going to be her last letter to me. She says she's done with her paper and she did very well and illustrated her paper with some of the things I had told her about African culture. But she says her parents are moving back to the city, that the farm had not worked out as planned. She also said she has become interested in Japanese haiku and was in search of new friends from Japan."

"Is that why you are looking sad like a dog whose juicy morsel fell on the sand? You should thank God for saving you from a relationship where each time the lady clears her throat you have to jump. Sit down and drink with us, forget your sorrows and let the devil be ashamed," Jekwu said.

We all laughed but Onwordi did not laugh with us, he walked away in a slight daze. From that time onwards we never saw him at Ambo's shop again. Some people who went to check in on him said they found him lying on his bed with Laura Williams's letters and picture on his chest as he stared up into the tin roof.

CHIMAMANDA NGOZI ADICHIE

· *Nigeria* ·

❖

HALF OF A YELLOW SUN

THE IGBO SAY that a mature eagle feather will always remain spotless.

· · ·

It was the kind of day in the middle of the rainy season when the sun felt like an orange flame placed close to my skin, yet it was raining, and I remembered when I was a child, when I would run around on days like this and sing songs about the dueling sun and rain, urging the sun to win. The lukewarm raindrops mixed with my sweat and ran down my face as I walked back to my hostel after the rally. I was still holding the placard that read *Remember the Massacres,* still marveling at my new—at our new—identity. It was late May, Ojukwu had just announced the secession, and we were no longer Nigerians. We were Biafrans.

When we gathered at the Freedom Square for the rally, thousands of us students shouted Igbo songs and swayed, river-like; somebody said that in the market outside our campus, the women were dancing, giving away groundnuts and mangoes. Nnamdi and I stood next to each other and our shoulders touched as we waved green dogonyaro branches and cardboard placards. Nnamdi's placard read *Secession Now.* Even though he was one of the student leaders, he chose to be with me in the crowd. The other leaders were in front carrying a coffin with NIGERIA written on it in white chalk. When they dug a shallow hole and buried the coffin, a cheer rose and snaked around the crowd, uniting us, elevating us, until it was one cheer, until we all became one.

I cheered loudly, although the coffin reminded me of Aunty Ifeka, Mama's half-sister, the woman whose breast I sucked because Mama's dried up after I was born. Aunty Ifeka was killed during the massacres in the North. So was Arize, her pregnant daughter. They must have cut open Arize's stomach and beheaded the baby first—it was what they did to the pregnant women. I didn't tell Nnamdi that I was thinking of Aunty Ifeka and Arize again. Not because I had lost only two relatives while he had lost three uncles and six cousins. But because he would caress my face and say, "I've told you, don't dwell on the massacres. Isn't it why we seceded? Biafra is born! Dwell on that instead. We will turn our pain into a mighty nation. We will turn our pain into the pride of Africa."

Nnamdi was like that; sometimes I looked at him and saw what he would have been two hundred years before: an Igbo warrior leading his hamlet in battle (but only a fair battle), shouting and charging with his fire-warmed machete, returning with the most heads lolling on sticks.

I was in front of my hostel when the rain stopped; the sun had won the fight. Inside the lounge, crowds of girls were singing. Girls I had seen struggle at the water pump and hit each other with plastic buckets, girls who had cut holes in each other's bras as they hung out to dry, now held hands and sang. Instead of "Nigeria we hail thee," they sang, "Biafra we hail thee." I joined them, singing, clapping, talking. We did not mention the massacres, the way Igbos had been hunted house to house, pulled from where they crouched on trees, by bright-eyed people screaming Jihad, screaming *nyamiri, nyamiri*. Instead, we talked about Ojukwu, how his speeches brought tears to our eyes and goose bumps to our skin, how easily his charisma would stand out among other leaders—Nkrumah would look like a plastic doll next to him. "*Imakwa,* Biafra has more doctors and lawyers than all of Black Africa!" somebody said. "Ah, Biafra will save Africa!" another said. We laughed, deliriously proud of people we would never even know, people who a month ago did not have the "ours" label as now.

We laughed more in the following weeks—we laughed when our expatriate lecturers went back to Britain and India and America, because even if war came, it would take us only one week to crush Nigeria. We laughed at the Nigerian navy ships blocking our ports, because the blockade could not possibly last. We laughed as we gathered under the gmelina trees to discuss Biafra's future foreign policy, as we took down the "University of Nigeria, Nsukka" sign and replaced it with "University of Biafra, Nsukka." Nnamdi hammered in the first nail. He was first, too, to join the Biafran Army, before the rest of his friends followed. I went with him to the army enlistment office, which still smelled of fresh paint, to collect his uniform. He looked so broad-shouldered in it, so capable, and later, I did not let him take it all off, I held on to the grainy khaki shirt as he moved inside me.

My life—our lives—had taken on a sheen. A sheen like patent leather. We all felt as though it was liquid steel, instead of blood, that flowed through our veins, as though we could stand barefoot over red-hot embers.

. . .

The Igbo say—who knows how water entered the stalk of a pumpkin?

. . .

I heard the guns from my hostel room. They sounded close, as though thunder was being funneled up from the lounge. Somebody was shouting outside with a loudspeaker. Evacuate now! Evacuate now! There was the sound of feet, frenzied feet, in the hallway. I threw things in a suitcase, nearly forgot my underwear in the drawer. As I left the hostel, I saw a girl's stylish sandal left lying on the stairs.

. . .

The air in Enugu smelled of rain and fresh grass and hope and new anthills. I watched as market traders and grandmothers and little boys hugged Nnamdi, caressed his army uniform. Justifiable heroism, Obi called it. Obi was thirteen, my bespectacled brother who read a book a day and went to the Advanced School for Gifted Children and was researching the African origin of Greek civilization. He didn't just touch Nnamdi's uniform, he wanted to try it on, wanted to know exactly what the guns sounded like. Mama invited Nnamdi over and made him a mango pie. "Your uniform is so debonair, darling," she said, and hung around him as though he was her son, as though she had not muttered that I was too young, that his family was not quite *suitable,* when we got engaged a year ago.

Papa suggested Nnamdi and I get married right away, so that Nnamdi could wear his uniform at the wedding and our first son could be named Biafrus. Papa was joking, of course, but perhaps because something had weighed on my chest since Nnamdi entered the army, I imagined having a child now. A child with skin the color of a polished mahogany desk, like Nnamdi's. When I told Nnamdi about this, about the distant longing somewhere inside me, he pricked his thumb, pricked mine, although he was not usually superstitious, and we smeared our blood together. Then we laughed because we were not even sure what the hell that meant exactly.

. . .

The Igbo say that the maker of the lion does not let the lion eat grass.

. . .

I watched Nnamdi go, watched until the red dust had covered his boot prints, and felt the moistness of pride on my skin, in my eyes. Pride at his smart olive uniform with the image of the sun rising halfway on the sleeve. It was the same symbol, half of a yellow sun, that was tacked onto the garish cotton tie Papa now wore to his new job at the War Research Directorate every day. Papa ignored all his other ties, the silk ones, the symbol-free ones. And Mama, elegant Mama with the manicured nails, sold some of her London-bought dresses and organized a women's group at St. Paul's that sewed for the soldiers. I joined the group; we sewed singlets and sang Igbo songs. Afterwards, Mama and I walked home (we didn't drive to save petrol) and when Papa came home in the evenings, during those slow months, we would sit in the verandah and eat fresh anara with groundnut paste and listen to Radio Biafra, the kerosene lamp casting amber shadows all around. Radio Biafra brought stories of victories, of Nigerian corpses lining the roads. And from the War Research Directorate, Papa brought stories of our people's genius: we made brake fluid from coconut oil, we created car engines from scrap metal, we refined crude oil in cooking pots, we had perfected a homegrown mine. The blockade would not deter us.

Often, we ended those evenings by telling each other, "We have a just cause," as though we did not already know. Necessary Affirmation, Obi called it.

It was on one of those evenings that a friend dropped by to say that Nnamdi's battalion had conquered Benin, that Nnamdi was fine. We toasted Nnamdi with palm wine. "To our Future Son-in-Law," Papa said, raising his mug towards me. Papa let Obi drink as much as he wanted. Papa was a Cognac man himself, but he couldn't find Rémy Martin even on the black market, because of the blockade. After a few mugs, Papa said, with his upper lip coated in white foam, that he preferred palm wine now, at least he didn't have to drink it in snifters. And we all laughed too loudly.

. . .

The Igbo say—the walking ground squirrel sometimes breaks into a trot, in case the need to run arises.

. . .

Enugu fell on the kind of day in the middle of the harmattan when the wind blew hard, carrying dust and bits of paper and dried leaves, covering hair and clothes with a fine brown film. Mama and I were cooking pepper soup—I cut up the tripe while Mama ground the peppers—when we heard the guns. At first I thought it was thunder, the rumbling thunder that preceded harmattan storms. It couldn't be the Federal guns because Radio Biafra said the Federals were far away, being driven back. But Papa dashed into the kitchen moments later, his cotton tie skewed. "Get in the car now!" he said. "Now! Our directorate is evacuating."

We didn't know what to take. Mama took her manicure kit, her small radio, clothes, the pot of half-cooked pepper soup wrapped in a dishtowel. I snatched a packet of crackers. Obi grabbed the books on the dining table. As we drove away in Papa's Peugeot, Mama said we would be back soon anyway, our troops would recover Enugu. So it didn't matter that all her lovely china was left behind, our radiogram, her new wig imported from Paris in the case that was such an unusual lavender color. "My leather-bound books," Obi added. I was grateful that nobody brought up the Biafran soldiers we saw dashing past, on the retreat. I didn't want to imagine Nnamdi like that, running like a chicken drenched by heavy rain.

Papa stopped the car often to wipe the dust off the windscreen, and he drove at a crawl, because of the crowds. Women with babies tied to their backs, pulling at toddlers, carrying pots on their heads. Men pulling goats and bicycles, carrying wood boxes and yams. Children, so many children. The dust swirled all around, like a see-through brown blanket. An exodus clothed in dusty hope. It took a while before it struck me that, like these people, we were now refugees.

. . .

The Igbo say that the place from where one wakes up is his home.

. . .

Papa's old friend, Akubueze, was a man with a sad smile whose greeting was "God Bless Biafra." He had lost all his children in the massacres. As he showed us the smoke-blackened kitchen and pit latrine and room with the stained walls, I wanted to cry. Not because of the room we would rent from Akubueze, but because of Akubueze. Because of the apology in his eyes. I placed our raffia sleeping mats at the corners of the room, next to our bags and food. But the radio stayed at the center of the room and we walked around it every day, listened to it, cleaned it. We sang along when the soldiers' Marching Songs were broadcast. *We are Biafrans, fighting for survival, in the name of Jesus, we shall conquer, hip hop, one two.* Sometimes the people in the yard joined us, our new neighbors. Singing meant that we did not have to wonder aloud about our house with the marble staircase and airy verandahs. Singing meant we did not have to acknowledge aloud that Enugu remained fallen and that the War Directorate was no longer paying salaries and what Papa got now was an *allowance.* Papa gave every note, even the white slip with his name and ID number printed in smudgy ink, to Mama. I would look at the money and think how much prettier than Nigerian pounds Biafran pounds were, the elegant writing, the bolder faces. But they could buy so little at the market, those Biafran pounds.

The market was a cluster of dusty, sparse tables. There were more flies than food, the flies buzzing thickly over the graying pieces of meat, the black-spotted bananas. The flies looked healthier, fresher, than the meat and fruits. I looked over everything, I insisted, as if it was the peacetime market and I still had the leisure that came with choice. In the end, I bought cassava, always, because it was the most filling and economical. Sickly tubers, the ones with grisly pink skin. We had never eaten those before. I told Mama, half-teasing, that they could be poisonous. And Mama laughed and said, "People are eating the peels now, honey. It used to be goat food."

. . .

The months crawled past and I noted them when my periods came, scant, more mud-colored than red now. I worried about Nnamdi, that he would not find us, that something would happen to him and nobody would know where to find me. I followed the news on Radio Biafra carefully, although Radio Nigeria intercepted so often now. Deliberate jamming, Obi said it was called. Radio Biafra described the thousands of Federal bodies floating on the Niger. Radio Nigeria listed the thousands of dead and defecting Biafran soldiers. I listened to both with equal attention, and afterwards, I created my own truths and inhabited them, believed them.

. . .

The Igbo say that unless a snake shows its venom, little children will use it for tying firewood.

. . .

Nnamdi appeared at our door on a dry-aired morning, with a scar above his eye and the skin of his face stretched too thin and his worn trousers barely staying on his waist. Mama dashed out to the market and bought three chicken necks and two wings, and fried them in a little palm oil. "Especially for Nnamdi," she said gaily. Mama, who used to make Coq au Vin without a cookbook.

I took Nnamdi to the nearby farm that had been harvested too early. All the farms looked that way now, raided at night, raided of corn so tender they had not yet formed kernels and yams so young they were barely the size of my fist. Harvest of desperation, Obi called it.

Nnamdi pulled me down to the ground, under an ukpaka tree. I could feel his bones through his skin. He scratched my back, bit my sweaty neck, held me down so hard I felt the sand pierce my skin. And he stayed inside me so long, so tightly, that I felt our hearts were pumping blood at the same rhythm. I wished in a twisted way that the war would never end so that it would always have this quality, this quality of nutmeg, tart and lasting. Afterwards, Nnamdi started to cry. I had never even considered that he could cry. He said the British were giving more arms to Nigeria, Nigeria had Russian planes and Egyptian pilots, the Americans didn't want to help us, we were still blockaded, his battalion was down to two men using one gun, some battalions had resorted to machetes and cutlasses. "Didn't they kill babies for being born Igbo, eh?" he asked.

I pressed my face to his, but he wouldn't stop crying. "Is there a God?" he asked me. "Is there a God?" So I held him close and listened to him cry, and listened to the shrilling of the crickets. He said goodbye two days later, holding me too long. Mama gave him a small bag of boiled rice.

I hoarded that memory, and every other memory of Nnamdi, used each sparingly. I used them most during the air raids, when the screeching *ka-ka-ka* of the anti-aircraft guns disrupted a hot afternoon and everybody in the yard dashed to the bunker—the room-sized hole in the ground covered with logs—and slid into the moist earth underneath. Exhilarating, Obi called it, even though he got scratches and cuts. I would smell the organic scent, like a freshly tilled farm, and watch the children crawl around looking for crickets and earthworms, until the bombing stopped. I would rub the soil between my fingers and savor thoughts of Nnamdi's teeth, tongue, voice.

. . .

The Igbo say—let us salute the deaf, for if the heavens don't hear, then the earth will hear.

. . .

So many things became transient, and more valuable. It was not that these things had value, it was that the ephemeral quality hanging over me, over life, gave value to them. And so I savored a plate of cornmeal, which tasted like cloth, because I might have to leave it and run into the bunker, because when I came out a neighbor may have eaten it, or given it to one of the children.

Obi suggested that we teach classes for those children, so many of them running around the yard chasing lizards. "They think bombings are normal," Obi said, shaking his head. He picked a cool spot under the kolanut tree for our classroom. I placed planks across cement blocks for chairs, a wooden sheet against the tree for a blackboard. I taught English, Obi taught Mathematics and History and the children did not whisper and giggle in his class as they did in mine. He seemed to hold them somehow, as he talked and gestured and scrawled on the board with charcoal (later he ran his hands over his sweaty face and left black patterns like a design). Perhaps it was that he mixed learning and playing—once he asked the children to role-play the Berlin conference; they became Europeans partitioning Africa, giving hills and rivers to each other although they didn't know where the hills and rivers were. Obi played Bismarck. "My contribution to the young Biafrans, our leaders of tomorrow," he said, glowing with mischief.

I laughed, because he seemed to forget that he, too, was a future Biafran leader. Sometimes even I forgot how young he was. "Do you remember when I used to half-chew your beef and then put it in your mouth so it would be easier for you to chew?" I teased. And Obi made a face and said he did not remember.

The classes were in the morning, before the afternoon sun turned fierce. After the classes, Obi and I joined the local militia—a mix of young people and married women and injured men—and went "combing," to root out Federal soldiers or Biafran saboteurs hiding in the bush although all we found were dried fruits and groundnuts. We talked about dead Nigerians, we talked about the braveness of the French and Tanzanians in supporting Biafra, the evil of the British. We did not talk about dead Biafrans. We talked about anti-kwash, too, how it really worked, how many children in the early stages of kwashiorkor had been cured. I knew that anti-kwash was absolute nonsense, those leaves were from a tree nobody used to eat, they filled the children's bellies but gave no nourishment, definitely no proteins. But we *needed* to believe stories like that. When you were stripped down to sickly cassava, you used everything else fiercely and selfishly—especially the ability to choose what to believe and what not to believe.

I enjoyed those stories we told, the lull of our voices. Until one day, we were at an abandoned farm wading through tall grass when we stumbled upon something. A body. I smelled it before I saw it, a smell that gagged me, suffocated me, a smell so bad it made me light-headed. "Hei! He's a Nigerian!" a woman said. The flies rose from the bloated body of the Nigerian soldier as we gathered round. His skin was ashy, his eyes were open, his tribal marks were thick eerie lines running across his swollen face. "I wish we had seen him alive," a young boy said. "*Nkakwu,* ugly rat," somebody else said. A young girl spit at the body. Vultures landed a few feet away. A woman vomited. Nobody suggested burying him. I stood there, dizzy from the smell and the buzzing flies and the heat, and wondered how he had died, what his life had been like. I wondered about his family. A wife, who would be looking outside, her eyes on the road, for news of her husband. Little children who would be told, "Papa will be home soon." A mother who had cried when he left. Brothers and sisters and cousins. I imagined the things he left behind—clothes, a prayer mat, a wooden cup used to drink kunu.

I started to cry.

Obi held me and looked at me with a calm disgust. "It was people like him who killed Aunty Ifeka," Obi said. "It was people like him who beheaded unborn babies."

I brushed Obi away and kept crying.

• • •

The Igbo say that a fish that does not swallow other fish does not grow fat.

• • •

There was no news of Nnamdi. When a neighbor heard from their son or husband in the front, I hung around their room for days willing their good fortune to myself. Nnamdi is fine, Obi said in a tone so normal I wanted to believe him. He said it often during those months of boiled cassava, months of moldy yams, months when we shared our dreams of vegetable oil and fish and salt.

I hid what little food we had because of the neighbors, wrapped in a mat and stuck behind the door. The neighbors hid their own food too. In the evenings, we all unwrapped our food and clustered in the kitchen, cooking and talking about salt. There was salt in Nigeria, salt was the reason our people were crossing the border to the other side, salt was the reason a woman down the road was said to have run out of her kitchen and tore her clothes off and rolled in the dirt, wailing. I sat on the kitchen floor and listened to the chatter and tried to remember what salt tasted like. It seemed surreal now, that we had a crystal saltshaker back home. That I had even wasted salt, rinsing away the clumpy bottom before re-filling the shaker. Fresh salt. I interspersed thoughts of Nnamdi with thoughts of salty food.

And when Akubueze told us that our old pastor, Father Damian, was working in a refugee camp in Amandugba, two towns away, I thought about salt. Akubueze was not sure, stories drifted around about so many people being at so many places. Still, I suggested to Mama that we go and see Father Damian. Mama said yes, we would go to see if he was well, it had been two long years since we saw him. I humored her and said it *had* been long—as though we still paid social calls. We did not say anything about the food that Caritas Internationalis sent to priests by secret night flights, the food that the priests gave away, the corned beef and glucose and dried milk. And salt.

· · ·

Father Damian was thinner, with hollows and shadows on his face. But he looked healthy next to the children in the refugee camp. Stick-thin children whose bones stuck out, so unnaturally, so sharply. Children with rust-colored hair and stomachs like balloons. Children whose eyes were swallowed deep in their faces. Father Damian introduced Mama and me to the other priests, Irish missionaries of the Holy Ghost, white men with sun-reddened skin and smiles so brave I wanted to tug at their faces and see if they were real. Father Damian talked a lot about his work, about the dying children, but Mama kept changing the subject.

It was so unlike her, something she would call *unmannered* if somebody else did it. Father Damian finally stopped talking about the children, about kwashiorkor, and he looked almost disappointed as he watched us leave, Mama holding the bag of salt and corned beef and fish powder he gave us.

Why was Father Damian telling us about those children? Mama shouted as we walked home. What can we do for them? I calmed her down, told her he probably just needed to talk to someone about his work and did she remember how he used to sing those silly, off-tune songs at church bazaars to make the children laugh?

But Mama kept shouting. And I too began shouting, the words tumbling out of my mouth. Why the hell did Father Damian tell us about those dying children, anyway? Did we need to know? Didn't we have enough to deal with?

. . .

Shouting. A man walked up the street, beating a metal gong, asking us to pray for the good white people who were flying food in for the relief center, the new one they set up in St. Johns. Not all white people were killers, gong, gong, gong, not all were arming the Nigerians, gong, gong, gong.

At the relief center, I fought hard, kicking through the crowds, risking the flogging militia. I lied, cajoled, begged. I spoke British-accented English, to show how educated I was, to distinguish me from the common villagers, and afterwards I felt tears building up, as though I only had to blink and they would flow down. But I didn't blink as I walked home, I kept my eyes roundly open, my hands tightly wrapped around whatever food I got. When I got food. Dried egg yolk. Dried milk. Dried Fish. Cornmeal.

The shell-shocked soldiers in filthy shirts roamed around the relief center, muttering gibberish, children running away from them. They followed me, first begging, then trying to snatch my food. I shoved at them and cursed them and spit in their direction. Once I shoved so hard one of the men fell down, and I didn't turn to see if he got up all right. I didn't want to imagine, either, that they had once been proud Biafran soldiers like Nnamdi.

✤

Perhaps it was the food from the relief center that made Obi sick, or all the other things we ate, the things we brushed blue mold from, or picked ants out of. He threw up, and when he was emptied, he still retched and clutched at his belly. Mama brought in an old bucket for him, helped him use it, took it out afterwards. I'm a chamber pot man, Obi joked. He still taught his classes but he talked less about Biafra and more about the past, like did I remember how Mama used to give herself facials with a paste of honey and milk? And did I remember the soursop tree in our backyard, how the yellow bees formed columns on it?

Mama went to Albatross hospital and dropped the names of all the famous doctors she had known in Enugu, so that the doctor would see her before the hundreds of women thronging the corridors. It worked, and he gave her diarrhea tablets. He could spare only five and told her to break each in two so they would last long enough to control Obi's diarrhea. Mama said she doubted that the "doctor" had even reached his fourth year in medical school, but this was Biafra two years into the war and medical students had to play doctor because the real doctors were cutting off arms and legs to keep people alive. Then Mama said that part of the roof of Albatross hospital had been blown off during an air raid. I didn't know what was funny about that but Obi laughed, and Mama joined in, and finally I did, too.

. . .

Obi was still sick, still in bed, when Ihuoma came running into our room, a woman whose daughter was lying in the yard inhaling a foul concoction of spices and urine that somebody said cured asthma. "The soldiers are coming," Ihuoma said. She was a simple woman, a market trader, the kind of woman who would have nothing in common with Mama before Biafra. But now, she and Mama plaited each other's hair every week. "Hurry," she said. "Bring Obi to the outer room, he can hide in the ceiling!" It took me a moment to understand, although Mama was already helping Obi up, rushing him out of the room. We had heard that the Biafran soldiers were conscripting young men, children really, and taking them to the front, that it had happened in the yard down our street a week ago, although Obi said he doubted they had really taken a twelve-year-old. We heard too that the mother of the boy was from Abakaliki, where people cut their hair when their children died, and after she watched them take her son, she took a razor and shaved all her hair off.

The soldiers came shortly after Obi and two other boys climbed into a hole in the ceiling, a hole that appeared when the wood gave way after a bombing. Four soldiers with bony bodies and tired eyes. I asked if they knew Nnamdi, if they'd heard of him, even though I knew they hadn't. The soldiers looked inside the latrine, asked Mama if she was sure she was not hiding anybody, because that would make her a saboteur and saboteurs were worse than Nigerians. Mama smiled at them, then used her old voice, the voice of when she hosted three-course dinners for Papa's friends, and offered them some water before they left.

Afterwards, Obi said he would enlist when he felt better. He owed it to Biafra and besides, fifteen-year-olds had fought in the Persian war. Before Mama left the room, she walked up to Obi and slapped his face so hard that I saw the immediate slender welts on his cheek.

• • •

The Igbo say that the chicken frowns at the cooking pot, and yet ignores the knife.

• • •

Mama and I were close to the bunker when we heard the anti-aircraft guns. "Good timing," Mama joked, and although I tried, I could not smile. My lips were too sore, the harmattan winds had dried them to a bloody crisp during our walk to the relief center and besides, we had not been lucky, we got no food.

Inside the bunker, people were shouting Lord, Jesus, God Almighty, Jehovah. A woman was crumpled next to me, holding her toddler in her arms. The bunker was dim, but I could see the crusty ringworm marks all over the toddler's body. Mama was looking around. "Where is Obi?" she asked, clutching my arm. "What is wrong with that boy, didn't he hear the guns?" Mama got up, saying she had to find Obi, saying the bombing was far away. But it wasn't, it was really close, loud, and I tried to hold Mama, to keep her still, but I was weak from the walk and hunger and Mama pushed past me and climbed out.

The explosion that followed shook something inside my ear loose, and I felt that if I bent my head sideways, something hard-soft like cartilage would fall out. I heard things breaking and falling above, cement walls and glass louvers and trees. I closed my eyes and thought of Nnamdi's voice, just his voice, until the bombing stopped and I scrambled out of the bunker. The bodies strewn across the street, some painfully close to the bunker entrance, were still quivering, writhing. They reminded me of the chickens our steward used to kill in Enugu, how they flapped around in the dust after their throats had been slit, over and over, before finally laying quiet. Dignity dance, Obi called it.

I was bawling as I stared at the bodies, all people I knew, trying to identify Mama and Obi. But they were not there. They were in the yard, Mama helping wash the wounded, Obi writing in the dust with his finger. Mama did not scold Obi for being so careless, and I did not rebuke Mama for dashing out like that either. I went into the kitchen to soak some dried cassava for dinner.

. . .

Obi died that night. Or maybe he died in the morning. I don't know. I simply know that when Papa tugged at him in the morning and then when Mama threw herself on him, he did not stir. I went over and shook him, shook him, shook him. He was cold.

"*Nwa m anwugo,*" Papa said, as though he had to say it aloud to believe it. Mama brought out her manicure kit and started to clip Obi's nails. "What are you doing?" Papa asked. He was crying. Not the kind of manly crying that is silence accompanied by tears. He was wailing, sobbing. I watched him, he seemed to swell before my eyes, the room was unsteady. Something was on my chest, something heavy like a jerry can full of water. I started to roll on the floor, to ease the weight. Outside, I heard shouting. Or was it inside? Was it Papa? Was it Papa saying *nwa m anwugo, nwa m anwugo.* Obi was dead. I grasped around, frantic, trying to remember Obi, to remember the concrete things about him. And I could not. My baby brother who made wisecracks and yet I could not remember any of them. I could not even remember anything he said the night before. I had felt that I had Obi for a long, long time and that I did not need to notice him, really notice him. He was there, I felt, he would always be there. I never had the fear that I had about Nnamdi, with Obi, the fear that I may mourn someday. And so I did not know how to mourn Obi, if I could mourn Obi. My hair was itching and I started to tear at it, felt the warm blood on my scalp, I tore some more and then more. With my hair littered on our floor, I wrapped my arms around myself and watched as Mama calmly filed Obi's nails.

. . .

There was something feverish about the days after Obi's death, something malarial, something so numbingly fast that it left me free to not feel. Even Obi's burial in the backyard was fast, although Papa spent hours fashioning a cross from old wood. After the neighbors and Father Damian and the crying children dispersed, Mama called the cross *shabby* and kicked it, broke it, flung the wood away.

Papa stopped going to the War Research Directorate and dropped his patriotic tie into the pit latrine, and day after day, week after week, we sat in front of our room—Papa, Mama and me—staring at the yard. The morning a woman from down the street dashed into our yard, I did not look up, until I heard her shouting. She was waving a green branch. Such a brilliant, wet-looking green. I wondered where she got that, the plants and trees around were scorched by January's harmattan sun, blown bare by the dusty winds. The earth was sallow.

The war is lost, Papa said. He didn't need to say it though, we already knew. We knew when Obi died. The neighbors were packing in a hurry, to go into the smaller villages because we had heard the Federal soldiers were coming with truckloads of whips. We got up to pack. It struck me how little we had, as we packed, and how we had stopped noticing how little we had.

. . .

The Igbo say that when a man falls, it is his god who has pushed him down.

✥

Nnamdi clutched my hand too tight at our wedding. He did everything with extra effort now, as if he was compensating for his amputated left arm, as if he was shielding his shame. Papa took photos, telling me to smile wider, telling Nnamdi not to slouch. But Papa slouched, himself, he had slouched since the war ended, since the bank gave him fifty Nigerian pounds for all the money he had in Biafra. And he had lost his house—our house with the marble staircase—because it was declared abandoned property and now a civil servant lived there, a woman who had threatened Mama with a fierce dog when Mama defied Papa and went to see her beloved house. All she wanted was our china and our radiogram, she told the woman. But the woman whistled for the dog.

"Wait," Mama said to Papa, and came over to fix my hat. She had made my wedding dress and sewn sequins onto a secondhand hat. After the wedding, we had pastries in a café and as we ate, Papa told me about the wedding cake he used to dream about for me, a pink multi-layered cake, so tall it would shield my face and Nnamdi's face and the cake-cutting photo would capture only the groomsman's face, only Obi's face.

I envied Papa, that he could talk about Obi like that. It was the year Obi would have turned seventeen, the year Nigeria changed from driving on the left hand side of the road to the right. We were Nigerians again.

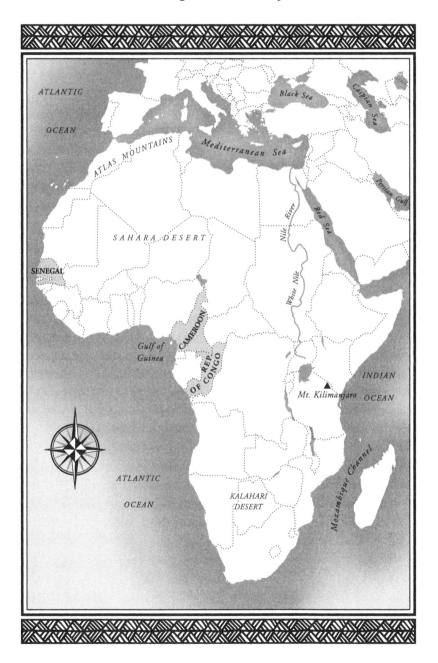

PATRICE NGANANG

· *Cameroon* ·

❖

THE SENGHOR COMPLEX

Translated by Cullen Goldblatt

Negro and Its Limits

I AM NOT a negro and I was never one. Whether it is written with or without a capital. The first time I heard the word used in relation to myself, I was twenty years old, and it was by then too late to become one. At the time I was in Germany. I was crossing the street, rushing a little, and bumped into a young man who threw out, "Neger." This was in Saarbrücken. I remember, rather than being dumbfounded, I was merely surprised. I didn't know the word had been addressed to me. I recount the episode here because Senghor, as we know from Jahn, translated Negritude into German as *Negersein*—the fact of being negro. Black, I was not that either until too late, and it too involved Germany, even though it was finally and especially the United States that taught me what black signifies. One could say that Senghor followed in his own way the path that I have just traced: the encounter with Germany, then the staggering discovery of African American texts, in particular the anthology *The New Negro* (1925), the impact of which on Senghor's own *Anthologie de la nouvelle poésie nègre* (1948) has not yet been adequately told. One method of verification: when I look in the mirror, I don't see a black. Cameroonian, yes, that I am and will remain. I have defined myself as that since childhood, and even today, adult, and having lived on three continents, I always return to what is for me a simple fact—as well as a passport—despite it not being a commitment. There is a bit of a habit of giving all Africans the same history, whether they be

Congolese, Nigerian, Senegalese, or Ghanaian, and regardless of their ages. The tendency is perhaps the reason why these defining preliminaries are important. That it be clear then: I never learned at school that my ancestors were Gaulois, but in fact quite the opposite; from very early on, I was made to feel the history of Cameroon in my body: my ancestors were Bamiléké[1]—and that I was therefore "Bamiléké," a "bams," "bami," "gros bami," "ngrafi," "cochon," "maquisard," "bosniaque," that I was one of "those people," as one still says today in Cameroon. I did not read *Mamadou et Bineta* at school, even if, from my father, who taught me to write, I had a CMII workbook for practicing French. A workbook I never used because the reading passages were "too hard," and did not help me resolve my own simple grammar problems. In short, the books I read at school, those that have stayed in my memory, had titles more along the lines of *Afrique mon Afrique* and *J'aime mon pays, le Cameroun*. It is simply that I was born in 1970, that symbolic year. And, according to my country's, Cameroon's, current statistics, more than half the population was born after 1970, that is to say, ten years after independence, and shares therefore, more or less, my past, and will perhaps understand the issues that I would like to articulate here.

It is that, for me, Senghor was always very complex. Perhaps because I never read him at school, but instead listened to him declaim his poems on the radio, especially his famous "Prière aux masques" and "Femme noire," in that sandy voice that still gives me goose flesh. During the same period, I listened to Rabemananjara, the last word of whose poem "Madagascar" is engraved in my memory, a horse's trot still reverberating in my ears: "Ma-da-gas-car." The slow fall of a ping-pong ball. The reason is simple: radio broadcasting in Cameroon having few soundtracks, the station would broadcast the few poems in its archives, then broadcast them, and broadcast them again. At five o'clock each evening, the national station. Even if his orchestral voice haunts me for a long time to come, Senghor will still appear complex to me. Perhaps because

---

1 It is important to note that the word "Bamiléké" does not exist in any of the languages of the groups who are designated by it, and thus it is not a designation intrinsic to the groups thus identified.

his collection of poems, *Poèmes,* published by Éditions du Seuil, is the first book that I bought with my own money, my economy of several weeks, augmented by my father so that I could reach the necessary sum of 1470 francs CFA. I bought Senghor of my own free will at the bookstore of Éditions Clé in Yaoundé in 1987—I know the date because I had by then bought a series of books, including Frantz Fanon's *Les Damnés de la terre* and *Peau noire, masques blancs;* and my then-teacher and mentor who later became my reader, Dassi Fosso, had advised me to write the date of purchase on the book's first page. Instead of writing the date, I drew the head of the Senegalese poet. Unlike my encounters with Césaire, whom we had read over and over in Lycée—*Une Tempête* in second year, *Cahier d'un retour au pays natal* in first, and *La Tragédie du roi Christophe* in terminale—Senghor was for me a private discovery. I discovered him because of his radio-broadcast voice, and between 1986 and 1988, I read my poems on the radio. So I sought out Senghor. Today, still, opening *Poèmes,* I realize that at that time, I always emphasized his postscript to *Éthiopiques*—"As the manatees drink at the source," especially the last two paragraphs, which I underlined a lot in pencil. The underlining does not surprise me, because these two paragraphs begin with this, "We have thus arrived at the last question: the diction of the poem." I underlined especially the sentences "This poem is a jazz score in which the performance is as important as the text," "Thus poems can be recited—I don't say declaimed—chanted or sang," and "The poem is not finished until it is made to chant, to be speech and music at once."[2] Rather practical reading, I would say, for a budding poet who, in a classic, looked for phrases like those of Rilke's *Letters to a Young Poet;* useful reading for a young writer to whom the poetry of the spoken word had been revealed by the radio, but to whom no one had ever given a practical handbook. During those formative years, did I ever read Senghor in any way other than poetic? I don't believe so.

Regarding writers of my generation, I usually say that Senghor is everyone's grandfather; certainly this signifies that he is not my father, be-

---

2   L. S. Senghor, "Comme les lamantins vont boire à la source," in *Poèmes* (Paris: Éditions du Seuil, 1974), pp. 165–66.

cause after all it is I who "sought out" him, to emphasize Ralph Ellison's term,[3] but above all, it means I always sought in Senghor's work "the architecture of the poem," the workmanship of poetic speech. And it is precisely here that Senghor's writing is rich, very few African writers having reflected so continuously, alongside their writing, upon the instruments of their writing. Faced with the masterly tomes of his reflections, *Liberté I, II, III,* etc., criticism establishes distinctions of importance, rickety stairs which set the poet against the president, the essayist against the poet, the theoretician of "African Socialism" against that of the "francophonie"; however, most of the time, happily, criticism does not divide his poetry into phases, the poet having begun to publish only quite late in life, after thirty. For me, however, all these aspects come together in a kind of edifice—thus in a complex—that intrigues and fascinates me, but does not evoke in me the repulsion that propelled Mongo Beti to write in all seriousness in "Conseils à un jeune écrivain francophone" (Advice for a Young Francophone Writer): "I swear, without the least confusion, that I do not read the works of this ex-president-poet; whatever I say about him, is what friends have told me."[4] I am a reader of Senghor, an observer of his complex, and when as an adult writer I passed from the diction of his writing to its meaning, from its meter to the labyrinth of his words, it became clear to me that the architecture of his poetry falls along four easily marked axes, all of which are obliterated before the simple fact that I am Cameroonian, that I am Bamiléké, as I mentioned at the beginning. The axes are these: first of all, identity as an analytical category; self-definition within a binary relationship which places the subject in opposition to the object; an evasion of the political paradox; and, finally, a relationship of too great an intimacy with Gaullism—I mean Gaullism and not France. I will analyze these four axes—that of logic, that of *épistèmè* (in the Foucaultian sense), that of ethics, and that of politics—step by step, gaze always fixed on our own violent times—before I draw conclusions, primarily through my relations, of which I

---

3   R. Ellison, *The Collected Essays* (New York: John Callahan, 1995), p. 185.

4   M. Beti, "Conseils à un jeune écrivain francophone ou les quarter premiers paradoxes de la francophonie ordinaire," dans *Africains, si vous parliez.* Homnispheres, 2005, 0.112.

have already named two—those relations whom I did not seek out, but who were givens on my path. Next, I will speak from the tradition in which these axes have situated Cameroon, the place from which I choose both to write about this country and to read Senghor.

Cameroonian Readings: Logic and Épistèmè

This is a fact: Senghor's poetry is made not only of form; it is also made of ideas, of concepts. It is similar to a structure of sand, cement, and water. Let us take identity. Is the fact that Senghor began to write during the triumphal period of racism—that of Nazism combined with colonialism—responsible for the clear grounding of his thought in the concepts of identity and belonging? He too was a son of his times, no doubt, and certainly it is still difficult to represent oneself other than in panegyrics: what it must have meant to be the first black *agrégé*[5]! Perhaps if one were to take into account what it meant to have been the only Black in the classroom, the only Black in the school, and perhaps even in the whole university, one could get some indication of what separates us from Senghor, we who were born in and grew up in Africa, and in a country where, without wanting it, we were in the majority. One would understand perhaps why a phrase like this one is closer to us in reality than are all the acts of Senghorian intellectual gymnastics: "a drive through the real Africa, among the real populace of the African world would have revealed that these millions had never at any time had cause to question the existence of their—Negritude."[6] Of course the question would be this: what is the "real Africa," but let us ask another first, for reference: who writes these lines? Soyinka, the mytho-poet of the road, who distinguishes Senghor's theoretical gesture—the product "by and for a tiny elite"[7]—from the creative activity of a pulsating Africa whose genius Soyinka himself attempts to grasp through history and myth. And I remember too his smile when I asked him last year in Han-

---

5   Trans. A rank of professor in the French university system.

6   W. Soyinka, *Myth, Literature and the African World* (Cambridge: Cambridge University Press, 1976), p. 135.

7   Ibid.

over, in what terms exactly had he put his phrase about the tiger, about how it does not proclaim its tigritude; I remember what he told me—after repeating his phrase and throwing in another reference to the eagle that does not proclaim its eagletude—that such preoccupations are known only to Francophone Africans. Is there a more polite way of saying that it is a non-issue? Notice, however, Soyinka's own reference to the "real Africa"—does this term not raise the same question as Senghor's Negritude? Truth in poetry is illusion, we know; however, is this issue not inscribed in the very logic of Negritude, in the fundamental essentialism of its quest? Too, Senghor speaks of *Wesen,* a concept he borrows from elsewhere, from German metaphysics and especially from ethnology, via his rather close reading of Leo Frobenius.

Negritude understood then as the *Wesen* of "the real Africa"? It is true that Senghor tries to escape into theory by creating, in *contre-coup,* the concept of the *"Civilisation de l'universel,"* perhaps most of all in order to counter Sartre's dialectics, set down in *Orphée noir,* that define Negritude as "anti-racist racism," and annihilates the concept with that same blow. Yet, does Senghor's "universal" abstraction quell the trembling that our era feels faced with any and all essentialisms? The representation of Africa as essentially black—here then is a mind game, the staggering limits of which our era can judge each day and night. And we know that Senghor's fertile mind had them to spare: "francité," "africanité," "arabité," "germanité," "latinité"—what says it better? By the same logic, we have watched the birth of "créolité," "antillanité," at the hands of Glissant, Chamoiseau, and their comrades. Blind in one eye, we are still applauding their creations. Have we not seen the same essentialism manufactured in Zaire, as well as in Togo, an "authenticité" that plunges these countries into diktat? Did we not see it, fraught with neologisms, among Ivorian intellectuals and writers, as Niangoran Porquet forged the "griotique" and then soon after "ivorité," which put the country into flames and blood?[8] As for "congolité," it has only just begun its macabre dance.

---

8 On the relationship between "negritudé" and "ivoirité" see U. Amoa, "Libre opinion—Lettre ouverte aux ivoiriens: Vive le changement . . . attention aux changements!" in *L'Inter,* Abidjan, January 3, 2000.

We can laugh today at Senghor's famous "negrité," but we should cry before the numerous offspring of his logic. In reality, we no longer need to criticize his Negritude, as Soyinka does, by opposing it with a so-called "real Africa" (which itself owes much to the logic of Negritude; which is elsewhere now called "neo-negritudiniste," according to another neologism, this time from Biodun Jeyifo). African history since the independences, our history, that is to say, is a better critic than any of us. Because, fundamentally, was Mugabe not armed with this vision of "negrité" when he took away the right of belonging to Africa from the whites of his country? Is Nadine Gordimer not an African writer? And, what of Coetzee then? We would ask Senghor. Moreover, since it is belonging we are speaking of, is it not for such a concept that the million Tutsis were massacred in Rwanda in 1994, subjected to the insane words "Go back to Egypt!" (the ancestry that Anta Diop had established between them, Ancient Egypt, and ourselves, having been turned against them). "Real Africa"? "Negrité"? A dangerous quest that has nonetheless damaged African intelligence in its essentialist pursuit of Negritude; a labyrinth where the masks of our by-the-kilo dead are dancing; a corridor of vampires in which even our most insightful writers are reeling drunkenly, beside our most cynical politicians! One day we will recognize this simple truth: Rwanda is the grave of Negritude. Until that day, we, children of violence and silence, are already living in this fact.

And from this evidence at the end of a long tunnel of night, Negritude appears to be rooted in an épistèmè that defines the African as other, fixing him or her in a binary relation (of conflict or of marriage, what does it matter?), of same and other, of subject and object. That this order of things is a heritage of Western thought, hundreds of contributions have already established; in their readings of Senghor's complex, they have not desisted from suggesting the intellectual falseness of his famous "kingdom of childhood." For us today, however, following Mudimbe's analysis, the subject/object relationship appears to be directly inherited from the colonial order that created an infinite number of dichotomies, of which Negritude itself as "a discourse of alterity," as Mudimbe's phrase goes, is one of the most vulgar manifestations. It becomes clear that this relationship, inscribed as it is in all its glory by

Sartre in his famous preface, *Orphée noir,* remains canonical. It is not only canonical in its logic (the figure of Narcissus is sufficient for that), but in its structure. It defines an idea's house and thus opens or closes various passageways and their possibilities. "I is an other," Rimbaud tells us; his phrase captures the paradoxical situation in which Negritude has placed us: I look at myself in the analytical mirror, the weapons Negritude has provided in my hands—and I see myself as the West's other! At the same time as I recognize the distortion of my face, I discover the chains on my ankles that bind me to that familiar dichotomy—same and other. In short, following the lead of colonial discourse, Negritude has African-ized Africa. How does one escape the violence that for Mudimbe is a "panacea" and for me, who was born in Cameroon, is the revelation of a conceptual prison? The lack of movement that has followed this frightening discovery, as much as it stuns me, shows that Negritude, in its épistèmè, has left us in a profound transcendental fall before the zigzags of our history, by erecting ethnology's assumptions inside of us; and leaving us unable, for example, to conceptualize the violence of which we are capable. It is incumbent upon us to create other paths, to see Negritude only as the prelude to a new order of intelligence, and to thus go beyond ethnology's othering dualism; we must open our minds to the "patience of philosophy," to begin to pay attention, to devote ourselves to the disassembling of our own reflection.

A question yet remains: why Senghor's complex, why the épistèmè of Negritude, remains so pervasive for writers today? No one would dare ask Victor Hugo to pay tribute to the classical era which he had rejected! Mudimbe, all the while drawing our attention to Ethiopian sources of knowledge, *Das Buch der weisen Philosophen nach dem Aethiopischen Untersucht* (1950), *Corpus Scriptorum Christianorum Orientalum* (1904), *Das Leben und die Sentenzen des Philosophen Secundus des Schweigsamen* (1887), opens a way for thought and imagination that, from Apuleius's Metamorphoses to Saint Augustine's *Confessions,* traces the possibilities of a kind of knowledge that is fixed on African terrain, far from the paradigm of race—but this possibility is not yet taken seriously today, erased as it is under the discursive hegemony of the ethnographic épistèmè. Let us not waste our time analyzing why this path was not taken: the history of ideas is always linked to that of power. Today the face of power in Africa is difficult to imagine without the hand of the West. It is strange, though, that embraced by the dialectic of subject/object, we would have been blind for so long in the face of the teleology of violence which has, since the independences, duped our countries—in Congo, in Bamileké country, and culminating first in Biafra, well before Rwanda, and today in Darfur; fixed in the épistème inherited from Negritude, African thought has been absent and asleep for too long, ignoring the explosive root, which, like a dangerous snake, runs through its land, and sporadically distorts its surface with seas of blood and millions of the dead. Conceived in a discursive system which places the African subject opposite the West and which elsewhere makes it into an object (and we would like to say, exonerates itself of any responsibility), African thought would not have suspected that such violence would make an African peasant cut his brother's neck with a machete, or stuff a banana tree branch in the vagina of his African sister, because "to kill is less work than to farm," as the genocidal peasants said in Hatzfeld's revelatory book; it would not have suspected the profound dehumanization that means the African calls his brother or sister, "cockroach"—or "frog," "bosnian," as happens in Cameroon. The Rwandan genocide is more than a warning to the hoax-makers of the "kingdom of childhood." We have already said it, but let us repeat it: Rwanda is the grave of Negritude.

Cameroonian Readings: Ethics and Politics

Today one can no longer think as if the genocide in Rwanda had not occurred. Genocide is, in essence, a State turned against its citizens, whom it annihilates. For us, then, if "Africa does not exist," as the Togolese Kossi Efoui said so well, it is because we were born in independent states, and our definition of citizen, and therefore of writer, is always situated in relation to this order of things. Our perspective on Senghor is, from this point of view, perhaps similar to the one from which Ludwig Borne viewed Goethe and which prompted him to write: "Goethe was always a servant of despots; his satire only deals skillfully with the small ones, while he wooed the big ones."[9] Harsh words which share the spirit of those Mongo Beti reserves for the poet-president. Their perspective, however, is our own, that of a citizen. It is from this point of view—citizen—that we are able to find Senghor's impossible paradox surprising. Let us clarify that we understand paradox in the purely etymological sense that prompts us to discover the neighbor—doxa, order. Here it is appropriate to remember Njabulo Ndebele's surprise, formulated into a question he posed at a symposium in Lagos in 1987, and which Alain Ricard relays to us: "Why are they so right-wing, these Francophones?[10] The answer, which Ricard searches for everywhere but in the evidence, is meanwhile inscribed in the terms of the question itself, in the word "Francophone," which is, as one remembers, a piece of the Senghorian inheritance. But perhaps we should again read Mongo Beti, who was absent from the symposium in question, an event where the Francophone presence was dominated by the dual faces of Ahmadou Kourouma and Sony Labou Tansi: "M. Senghor did not fear, since then, supporting books which presented militants or men of politics. It is true that these works expressed, always more or less hypocritically, approval of the African powers which were themselves favorable to the Western power dear to M. Senghor."[11] Ndebele, whose thinking was rooted in that of Beti, was surprised at the old relationship between art and politics, and the claim to an apolitical place for the artist which Senghor (who, one forgets too easily, never escaped the realm of politics from the time of his arrival in Paris in 1928) was suspected of having made in his defense of *L'Enfant noir.* In their shared concerns, however, Ndebele and Beti question less the apolitical place of art, because such a place does not exist (and certainly not in the backyard of the poet-president), than they question the ethics of the writer in the political: the writer's choice, and therefore, the morality of her art.

The State or the citizen? We would say that, as President, Senghor the poet was de facto the first citizen of his country; but perhaps we would

---

9   L. Borne, cited in V. Zmegac, *Geschichte der deutschen Literatur vom 18. Jahrhundert bis zur Gegenwart* (Koenigstein: Athenaeum Vg., 1984), p. 283.

10   A. Ricard, *La Formule Bardey. Voyages africains* (Bordeaux: Confluences, 2005), p. 196.

11   M. Beti, "Conseils à un jeune écrivain francophone," op cit., p. 112.

have enough shame to recognize a sophism in this response, because the place of writing, as we saw, even if that writing was black, would always be anchored firmly in the pocket of the State. A verse reveals a vision of the world as much as a grammar, and that of Senghor shows us a symbiotic relationship between the writer and his State. And so the geographies of lost civilizations align themselves appropriately (read: La Civilisation Nègre); and dot our field of vision with their infinite repetitions—"Kingdoms" of "Ancestral Africa" (read: Kingdom of Sine)—and the heroes of a mythical Africa multiply, among which the personage of "Prince" (read: Chaka) illuminates our tragedy, as if he had not committed genocide, this dear Chaka, exonerated by his singular blackness; and now add the face of power, of force: the energy is expressed by the "warrior" and the "athlete," and the "griot" (read: "Djali") provides the more enigmatic face. Wrote Senghor: "I say it clearly: I am Djali."[12] The gesture of his celebratory poetry is regal: it does not know self-doubt; it is not attacked by this line which ceaselessly gnaws at the heart of our spirit and makes the stinking garbage cans of our lives crumble before us. On the contrary, we see the Senghorian poem elaborating upon a philosophical tradition that, via ethnophilosophy, like that of Alexis Kagame, searches for the "philosophical Bantu," but leaves us with no guard against the genocides which torpedo our countries; we see the emergence of a historiography which, in the words of Hampaté Bâ ("when an old man dies, a library burns"), has clearly chosen its camp (that is, between that of the citizen and that of the State), and, in turning towards the Africa of the elders on a continent which is again selling its youth, we see the unfolding of an Africa that, through "Djali," has chosen to rewrite the continent's history to satisfy the "virile" powerful, this in an Africa that belongs to our mothers, wives, and sisters as well; we see a vision of writing which allows no place for the thousand gangrenes that gnaw the continent's very heart—today in the form of AIDS, which ravages its young people, and condemns its future to malaria. Standing before the expanse of a continent that he wants blackened, faced with the sporadic multiplying of cadavers, and the raging of

---

12 L. S. Senghor, "L'Absente," in *Poèmes,* op cit., p. 108.

the virus, the uncontrollable soaring of famine, and the culture of geno-cidal impunity, "Djali" says "Greatness" and, of necessity, invents it to the satisfaction of his king. The evasion of our history's paradox is a re-fusal to see an Africa which is obstinately killing itself; and this suicide lies as much a condemnation of the majorities of the population (women, young people, the poor . . .) to powerlessness as it lies in the plunging of the continent's intelligentsia into the "ancestral past," when the real stakes of the continent—its young people, we say it daily—is its future. The patron of "Djali" is the king, the "Prince"; now his power feeds on violence. "Universities today, particularly in Africa, have be-come the modern patrons for the artist,"[13] Ngūgī wa Thiong'o reminds us. Why, more than the Senghorian doxa, is it the citizen-place of writ-ing that emerges from these words, that nudges our intelligence? Per-haps, because, in the meantime, we learned to see the path to our safety in our empowerment—empowerment which yields all knowledge—and thus, to situate the promise of our recovered dignity less in celebra-tion than in skepticism.

The choice of skepticism over celebration is already a politics of writing. The most rectilinear Senghorian verse, in its choice of celebration and of "Djali" as the symbol of poet, is also itself political. We mean political in the sense of articulating the foundational language of a community. For Senghor, the mortar of community is fundamentally friendship. Few poets have cultivated friendship to the extent Senghor did, his re-lationship with Césaire being one of the most mythic. Senghor's poem is thus often epistolary, addressed to a friend; who, though, would have us read the letters of his actual exchanges with all these people? What editor would have the good fortune to publish the *Correspondances com-plètes* of Senghor? We are still waiting with his poems in our hands, poems that are little islands expressing form as much as idea, idea that is a labyrinth of human relationships. The central trait of this subterra-nean friendship in his poem, even judged only by its effect, is the intel-

---

13 Ngūgī wa Thiong'o, *Decolonizing the Mind* (London: J. Currey; Nairobi: Heinemann Kenya, 1986), p. vii.

ligent marriage between private and public. Some names leap to mind here—among them Pompidou, De Gaulle, and Eboué in particular—and convey a certain orientation, a manner of organizing the political, and express in their way a fidelity to a tradition, at the same time as they reveal a Senghor who was Gaullist from the very beginning, even in those times when Senegal, and the AOF (French West Africa), was not.

It would take too many words to sum up a political adventure lasting close to forty years, with all its contradictions, its resumptions, its erasures, its successes, its promises and elegies, among which the Senegalese democracy, the oldest of the continent, is certainly the most celebrated. Indeed, one would need too many words to capture a friendship that was formed as much on the benches of Lycée Louis-le-Grand and in the prison camps of Germany, as in the corridors of the French National Assembly, before revealing itself in the total subjugation of a country, Senegal, to French interests. For us, meanwhile, understood from the red earth of Bamileké country—which, in 1940, added its sons to the forty thousand men which a resisting France received from the AEF (American Expeditionary Force) in order to constitute the army it needed to free itself from under the German boot, and which harvested the flowers of rage between 1956 and 1970—understood from this rebellious land that in 1958 aligned itself with the tradition of Sékou Touré's "No," deciding, logically, to go "into the bush" under the leadership of Um Nyobé, Ernest Ouandie, Félix Moumié, the vengeful shadow of Gaullism covers Senghorian friendships with a mantle of blood. Considering the war of liberation that then shook Cameroon, the voices of which are already rising, fortunately, to tell of the genocide and to accuse France[14] directly, the existence of the "amitié francafricaine" (what France called the "Union Française," the "Francophonie" as Senghor would soon have it, or "Françafrique" as François-Xavier termed it) is truly remarkable.

✤

---

14 "La France accusée de genocide," in *Mutations,* Yaoundé, June 6, 2006 [www .quotidienmutations.net/mutations/32.php?subaction=showfull&id=1149568971&archive=& start_from=&ucat+32&].

One would ask oneself at times why French-speaking Africans have this relationship of "fraternelle amitié" with their former colonizer, a relationship which indeed surprises observers, France being, with its fourteen thousand soldiers stationed in Africa—of which twelve hundred are in Senegal—the Western country which has by far the largest number of military bases on the continent today, and which, long after the time of the French Colonial Army, still refuses to "decolonize itself,"[15] as Mbembe says. Always, Senghor will be at the center of this surprise, less as an enigma than as the epitome of a way of doing politics; the legacy of a poet of the "amitié francafricaine." Perhaps it is necessary, in the tradition of W.E.B. Du Bois, of whom Senghor was a fervent reader, and who in his famous *The Souls of Black Folk* asks, "Would America be America without her Negro people"; perhaps it is necessary to begin to ask ourselves what France would be without Africa; and especially what France would be without its African front, and thus, without the "amitié africaine" of these straw men, Francophonie having become today the ultimate bastion of tyranny in Africa. Certainly Senghor can do nothing about the way of doing politics, although he himself began the tradition. Let us look for a moment on the faces of infamy: Obiang Nguema of Equatorial Guinea with his twenty-seven years; Paul Biya, President of Cameroon, who last November could count twenty-four years in power and promised his country twenty years more; President of the Republic of Congo, Sassou Nguesso, is now in his twenty-fourth year in power; Ben Ali of Tunisia, who counts twenty-one years; Blaise Compaoré of Burkina Faso with nineteen years; but also the President of Chad, Idriss Déby, who with sixteen years in power has just won in elections which he did not even need to rig, it being a given that he also ran the campaign against himself. Let us stop at sixteen years, because it is the limit of a generation, African young people making up more than half of its population, the very ones that French soldiers killed in front of the Hôtel Ivoire in Abidjan on November 9, 2004. But we must add to this shameful list the names of those budding potentates, the sons

---

15   A. Mbembe, "La France et l'Afrique: décoloniser sans s'auto-décoloniser," in *Le Messager,* September 27, 2005 [www.lemessager.net/details_articles.php?code=109&code_art=8290].

who captured power upon the death of their father: Kabila Jr. of the RDC, then Faure Gnassingbé, who proved last year that a Constitution is not worth the paper it is written upon, and took the presidential seat, which his father had occupied for thirty-nine years, at gunpoint. How to express further the hideous face of "l'amitié francafricaine," if not by adding that, in supporting Habyarimana—President of Rwanda before 1994, "ami de la France" in power for twenty-one years—Paris would find itself implicated in a genocide?

Beyond Senghor: The Lesson of the Falls of Metche

Oh, it was not the first time. For us, Rwanda was a metaphor that articulated the limits of the politics of our time: a revelation of the teleology of violence that turned our path into a volcano of blood. I remember, during a reading tour in March 2005 in Bamileké country, on the road to Bafoussam in western Cameroon, meeting a procession of men and women going towards the Falls of Metche. The place was covered with kola nuts, with palm oil and pieces of broken calabash, the components of all Bamileké sacrifices. Intrigued by their dignified gestures, which, if I was a son of Senghor, I would connect to evidence of "Ancestral Africa," I asked them what was happening. "We've just made offerings to our relatives killed by the French in '60." They were my age, these people, and thus, like me, had not lived through those years, but their actions displayed the depth of their conviction. "Why?" I asked. Their response: "So that they rest in peace." My compatriots thus rewrote our history, in its deepest paradox, because the ones whom they wished would rest in peace were shot down by people such as a certain Colonel Lamberton, who was not afraid to say that Bamilekés "are an irritating pebble" in the foot of Cameroon. The shrieking and clattering of bullets covered by the sound of waterfalls, the bodies thrown into the Metche river, all had been forgotten. They were thus "unburied dead" in a country which believes if a corpse is not returned to the earth, its soul will eternally haunt the sky of the living. The fact that since 2005 an Association of Cameroonian Veterans (ASVECAM) has formed, reuniting more than two hundred "former *maquisards*" from the leaden years of 1956–1970, is more than just laudable. It bears the accusation of French genocide in Cameroon, and it bears the demand for reparations and for recognition of the historic importance[16] of their combat, so potent in the silence of our families. Fortunately, Mbembe's research on the maquis[17] of the Sanaga-Maritime,[18] and, before him, the anger of Mongo Beti in *Main basse sur le Cameroon* (in our time banned in France), exposed the criminal dimensions of the French presence in Cameroon's lower country and in the region of my origins, in Bamileké country. The importance of this history, of this mute violence, is not only that it is the root of Cameroon's present, those killed being those who first demanded the independence of and reunification of Cameroon—a fact that still defines our country—the importance of this history also derives from it being the expression of the Cameroonian people's critical intelligence; it is at the foundation of what I called a "Cameroonian reading" of Senghor.

It is this Cameroonian reading that guided the four axes of my analysis of the "Senghor complex," and which, even if it is at the source of Cameroonian literary, philosophical, and historiographical inspiration, is not yet acknowledged in school curriculum, is in fact entirely absent from the official history and pedagogy of Cameroon. Because, if this critical intelligence teaches us the truth, then my country's official history, since 1914 at least, is a cloth woven of appalling lies. Such a critical intelligence reminds us that Cameroon, after 1916 with the German defeat, was "la colonie de personne,"[19] let alone that of France, but was a country placed by the League of Nations under "a joint mandate," and by its successor the United Nations under the "double tutelage" of England and France. Such critical intelligence also informs us that, along with Algeria, Cameroon under French tutelage obtained its indepen-

---

16 "Cameroun: Lutte d'indépendance: les vétérans camerounais exigent des réparations," in *Le Messager,* Douala, June 2, 2006 [http://fr.allafrica.com/stories/200606020628.html].

17 Trans. "Resistance movement," here specifically that of '56–70.

18 A. Mbembe, *La Naissance du maquis dans le Sud-Cameroun, 1920–1960* (Paris: Karthala, 1996), p. 438.

19 Trans. "Nobody's colony." Slogan of the UPC before 1960. Note that many Cameroonians continue to write the name of the country with "K," as in the German "Kamerun," to mark this moment of rupture.

dence through bloodshed, and that Cameroon under English tutelage was included in Nigeria and independent in 1961; so the "Cameroon" we know obtained its independence twice—from France and from England. This intelligence reminds us that those who obtained Cameroon's independence under French tutelage, Ahidjo and his clique, were not beaten for it, worse, they were formally opposed to independence, and thus were rewarded for a battle that they had not fought, because of the simple fact of their "fraternelle amitié" with France. This intelligence also tells us that Cameroon today is not entirely "francophone," but instead is "bilingual." These rewritings of the country's history—and we must understand these to include the work of Mongo Beti as well as that of Bernard Fonlon, Marcien Towa, Jean-Marc Ela, Eboussi Boulaga, and of course that of Achille Mbembe—have in the meantime hollowed a deep intelligence from which today it is easy to write, when one is a Cameroonian author.

To think with this critical intelligence means to be anti-Senghorian; the logic of the Cameroonian reading which stems from it is necessarily opposed to Senghor's essentialist logic, to his "servitude," as Marcien Towa names it so precisely, because the character of this reading is full of eruptive passion and reverence for the unburied dead at the Falls of Metche, and for all the dead "Maquis." The épistèmè of this reading disrupts Senghor's ethnographic dualism using a radical critique of ethnophilosophy and Eboussi Boulaga's work on the "bantou problematique." And the ethics of such a reading distances it from the language of "Djali" when, in the company of Jean-Marc Ela, "the Priest in the Bou-Bou," we look for knowledge in what is whispered, for wisdom in the fragile space of "political beginners" and for "empowerment" in the ways that "little people" do things; when in these ways we search for truths, for the logics of history "from the bottom." Its politics, finally, clearly describes "l'amitié francafricaine" as the straitjacket of all Cameroonians who are, and want to think of themselves as, "bilingual," in the tradition of Bernard Fonlon, if there is not to be another undertow of the "postcolony," as Achille Mbembe names it. Yet these Cameroonian disruptions of Senghor's complex would be meaningless if we did not listen to them in the interstices of this time of violence, which since

1956 (the year which began the insurrection of the UPC (Union of the Peoples of Cameroon) and continued until 1970 (the year when Ouandie was stopped) has opposed the intellectual tradition that Cameroon claims as its critical intelligence with the official statements of a puppet regime, no, rather a regime imposed by France and its henchmen; if these disruptions are not read with the knowledge of the genocidal root at the heart of Cameroon, genocide which, they will one day say, is our Saint Bartholomew; if they are not read in close relation to the thousands of unburied dead whose absent tombstone is still today the constitutive stone of Cameroon. Many times we have said that Rwanda is the grave of Negritude. With genocide in our land, in the country of my origins, Bamileké country, it is difficult to pull words from us, words that for Senghor amounted only to applause, because we know that villages—my father's among them, Bazou—were razed. We know houses were treated with napalm, that thousands of people were killed, and that still today, corpses turn over inside our parents' silence, all as in the numerous enmities that strangely compose the matrix of Cameroonian peace. How to write the place of the "Civilisations Ancestrales" when we have the violence and silence of forty years to manage, and what is our country's State that it has orchestrated this violence and this silence? When we hold in our hands the falsification of a million lives erased by the logic of the Cameroonian State, which does not only usurp our history, but also imposes itself as the historian of our lives, which denies the dead who still swim in our rivers, and which has forbidden us for forty years to speak their names in public? When we discover that the *maquisards*—who were dead at the time of our birth, but who inspire us because they died for our red land—when we discover that when they were buried it was inside reinforced concrete? For me, the difficulty with Senghor will always be that, in the thousand pages of his writings, despite the length of his life and the reach of his voice, he did not demand justice for the dead who haunt our lives, for those who endure, believing themselves hidden, but sat down too quickly beside their assassins. More than his surfeit of writing, it is his silence that for me remains complex.

ALAIN MABANCKOU

· *Congo* ·

✧

from BROKEN GLASS

LET'S SAY THE boss of the bar *Credit Gone Away* gave me this notebook to fill, he's convinced that I—Broken Glass—can turn out a book, because one day, for a laugh, I told him about this famous writer who drank like a fish, and had to be picked up off the street when he got drunk, which shows you should never joke with the boss, he takes everything literally, when he gave me this notebook he said from the start it was only for him, no one else would read it, and when I asked why he was so set on this notebook, he said he didn't want *Credit Gone Away* just to vanish one day, and added that people in this country have no sense of the importance of memory, that the days when grandmothers reminisced from their death beds were gone now, this is the age of the written word, that's all that's left, the spoken word's just black smoke, wild cat's piss, the boss of *Credit Gone Away* doesn't like ready made phrases like *"in Africa, when an old person dies, a library burns,"* every time he hears that worn out cliché he gets mad, he'll say *"depends which old person, don't talk crap, I only trust what's written down,"* so I thought I'd jot a few things down here from time to time, just to make him happy, though I'm not sure what I'm saying, I admit I've begun to quite enjoy it, I won't tell him that, though, he'll get ideas and start to push me to do more and more, and I want to be free to write when I want, when I can, there's nothing worse than forced labour, I'm not his slave, I'm writing this for myself as well, that's why I wouldn't want to be in his shoes when he reads these pages, I don't intend to spare him or anyone else, by the time he reads this, though, I'll no longer be a client of his bar, I'll be dragging my bag of bones about some other place, just slip him the document quietly before I go, saying "mission accomplished."

I'll start by describing the row that broke out when the bar first opened, explain a bit about the sufferings of the boss, some people wanted to see him taking his final breath, drawing up his Judas testament, it began with the Church people, who, seeing their Sunday congregations had dwindled, launched a holy war, flinging their Jerusalem bibles at the door of *Credit Gone Away*, saying if things went on like this it would be the end of Sunday mass in our quartier, there'd be no more trances during the singing, no more Holy Spirit descending on the Trois-Cents, no more crispy black wafers, no more sweet wine, the blood of Christ, no more choir boys, no more pious sisters, no more candles, no more alms, no more first communion, no more second communion, no more catechism, no more baptism, no more anything, and everyone would go straight to hell, and after that the Weekend-and-bank-holiday-cuckolds Club waded in, claiming it was largely due to *Credit Gone Away* that their wives no longer cooked for them properly, or respected them as wives did in the old days, they said respect was important, that no one respects a husband like a wife does, that's always been the way of things, ever since Adam and Eve, and as good family men they saw no reason to change, let their wives continue to grovel and cringe, to follow men's orders, all this they said, but it had no effect, and then we had threats from some old club of ex-alcoholics, who'd gone over to water, Fanta, Pulp'Orange, syrup, Senegalese jungle juice, grapefruit juice and contraband Cola-lite traded for hashish in Nigeria, a righteous band of brothers who set siege to the bar for forty days and forty nights, but again all in vain, and then there was some mystical action from the guardians of traditional moral values, the tribal leaders with their gris-gris, which they flung at the door of the bar, casting curses at the boss of *Credit Gone Away*, summoning up the voices of the dead, bringing forth prophecies, saying the barkeeper would die a slow and painful death, they would nudge him gently towards his own scaffold, but that didn't work either, and finally there was direct action from a group of thugs who were paid by some old codgers from the quartier, nostalgic for the days of the Case de Gaulle, for the life of a houseboy, the life of the faithful Negro with his service medal, for the days of the Colonial Exhibition and the Negro Balls, with Josephine Baker leaping about in a skirt made out of bananas, and these paragons of respectability set snares without end for the boss, with their thugs in hoods who came at the dead of night, at the darkest hour, armed with iron bars from Zanzibar, with clubs and cudgels from mediaeval Christendom, poisoned spears from the time of Chaka Zulu, sickles and hammers from the Communist bloc, catapults from the Hundred Years War, Gallic bill hooks, pygmy hoes, Molotov cocktails from May '68, machetes left over from a killing spree in Rwanda, slings from the famous fight between David and Goliath, with all this heavy arsenal they came, but again, in vain, though they managed to destroy one part of the bar, and it was the talk of the town, and all over the papers, *La Rue Qui Meurt, La Semaine Africaine, Mwinda, Mouyondzi Tribune,* tourists even came from neighbouring countries to get a close look, like pilgrims at the Wailing Wall, taking masses of photos, like tourists, I don't know what for, but even so, they took photos, and some of them even came from our own town, people who'd never set foot in the Trois-Cents before, and were amazed to discover it, and wondered how on earth people could live quite happily surrounded by rubbish, pools of stagnant water, the carcasses of domestic animals, burned out vehicles, slime, dung, gaping holes in the roads, houses on the point of collapse, and our barman gave interviews all over the place, our barman became a martyr overnight, and our barman sprang up on every tv channel overnight, and spoke in the *lingala* of the north, in the *munukutuba* of the people of the Mayombe forest, in the *bembé* of the inhabitants of the bridge of Mouloukoulu, who settle all their disputes with a knife, and now everybody knew him, suddenly he was famous, people felt sorry for him, they wanted to help him, and even sent letters of support and petitions on behalf of the good guy they started to call "The Stubborn Snail," but the ones who really backed him were the drunks, who always stay loyal till the last bottle runs dry, and they decided to strike back and rolled up their sleeves to put right the damage caused by the people nostalgic for the days of the Colonial Exhibition, the Case de Gaulle, Josephine Baker's Negro Balls, and for some this trivial matter became a national issue, they called it "the *Credit Gone Away* Affair," the government discussed it in cabinet, and certain leading politicians called for its immediate and permanent closure, while others opposed such a move, for scarcely more convincing reasons, and the country suddenly found itself divided over this petty spat until, with the authority and wisdom for which he became renowned, the Minister for Agriculture, Commerce and Small and Large Businesses, Albert Zou Loukia, raised his voice in a memorable contribution to the debate, a contribution now regarded in these parts as one of the finest political speeches ever made, Minister Zou Loukia spoke, saying several times, "I accuse, I accuse," a remark so stupifyingly brilliant that at the slightest excuse—a minor dispute, or some slight injustice—people in the street started saying "I accuse," and even the head of government told his spokesman that the Minister for Agriculture was a fine speaker, and that his popular catch-phrase, "I accuse," would go down in history, and the Prime Minister promised that in the next reshuffle the Minister for Agriculture would be given the portfolio for Culture, all you had to do was cross out the first four letters of "agriculture," and to this very day it is widely agreed that the minister's speech was quite brilliant, quoting entire pages from books by the kind of great writers people like to quote at the dinner table, sweating as he always did when he was proud of having seduced an audience with his erudition, and that is how he came to defend *Credit Gone Away,* first praising the initiative of The Stubborn Snail, who he knew very well as they'd been at primary school together, and then summing up by saying—I quote from memory: *"Ladies and Gentlemen of Cabinet, I accuse, I wish to distance myself from our current moribund social climate, I refuse to condone this witch hunt by my presence in the government, I accuse the shabby treatment meted out to a man who has done no more than draw up a route map for his own existence, I accuse the cowardly and retrograde machinations we have witnessed in recent times, I accuse the uncivil nature of these barbarous acts, orchestrated by men of bad faith, I accuse the indecency and insubordination which have become common currency in this country, I accuse the sly complicity of all those who arm the thugs, I accuse man's contempt for his fellow man, the want of tolerance, the abandon of our values, the rising tide of hatred, the inertia of the individual conscience, the slimy toads in our midst and all around us, yes, Ladies and Gentlemen of Cabinet, just look at how the Trois-Cents has become a sleepless fortress, with a face of stone, while the man we now call Stubborn Snail, quite apart from the fact that he's an old school friend of mine, and a very intelligent man, this man who today is being hounded is the victim of a cabal, Ladies and Gentlemen of Cabinet, let us concentrate instead on the pursuit of real criminals, whereby I accuse those who with impunity paralyse the proper function of our institutions, those who openly break the chain of solidarity which we have inherited from our ancestors, the Bantu, I tell you the only crime of the Stubborn Snail is to have shown his fellow countrymen that each one of us, in his own way, can contribute to the transformation of human nature, just as the great Saint-Exupéry has shown us in his work 'Wind, Sand and Stars' and that is why I accuse, and will go on accusing forever."*

The day after Minister Zou Loukia's speech, the President of the Republic himself, Adrien Lokouta Eleki Mingi, flew into a rage, stamping his favourite daily dessert of grapes beneath his feet, and we were informed by Radio-Curbside FM that President Adrien Lokouta Eleki Mingi, who also happened to be general of the armies, was jealous of the Minister for Agriculture's phrase—"I accuse," indeed, he wished he had said it himself, and couldn't understand why his own advisers hadn't come up with a similarly short but snappy catch-phrase, instead of feeding him turgid set pieces along the lines of *"All things, like the Sun, rise on the distant horizon and set each evening over the majestic Congo river,"* so President Adrien Lokouta Eleki Mingi, in his vexation, mortification, degradation, humiliation and frustration, called a meeting of the supposedly devoted bunch of Negroes in his cabinet and bid them slave as they'd never slaved before, he was through with turgid set pieces dressed up in so-called lyrical language, and the Negroes in his cabinet leaped to attention and lined up, from the smallest to the tallest, like the Daltons in Lucky Luke, when he's tracking them through the cactus plains of the Wild West, and the Negroes all said as one man "yes sir, Commandant sir," when in fact President Adrien Lokouta Eleki Mingi was a general of the armies, and was longing for civil war to break out between north and south so he could write his war memoirs and give them the modest title "Memoirs of Hadrien," and the President and General of the armies called on them to find him a phrase that would be remembered by posterity as Minister Zou Loukia's "I accuse" would be, and the Negroes in the presidential cabinet worked all night long, behind closed doors, opening up and looking through—for the first time ever—encyclopaedias which stood gathering dust on the presidential bookshelves, they looked in large books with tiny writing, they worked their way back to the dawn of time, back through the age of some guy called Gutenberg, and back through the age of Egyptian hieroglyphics as far back as the writings of some Chinaman who it seems had a lot to say about the art of war and was supposed to have been alive in the days before anyone knew that Christ was going to be born by the power of the Holy Spirit and lay down his life for us sinners, but Adrien's Negroes could find nothing as good as Minister Zou Loukia's "I accuse," so the President and General of the armies threatened to sack the entire cabinet, unless they found him a phrase for posterity, and said: "Why should I go on paying a bunch of idiots who can't find me a decent enduring and memorable slogan, I'm warning you now, if I don't have my slogan by the time the cock crows tomorrow at dawn, heads will roll like rotten mangoes, that's all you are, the lot of you, rotten mangoes, let me tell you, you can start packing now, go into exile in some Catholic country, take your pick, exile or death, d'you hear me, starting now, no one leaves this palace as of this moment, I'm going to sit in my office and I don't want to pick up even the slightest whiff of coffee, not to mention cigars, Cohibas or Montecristos, there'll be no water, no sandwiches, nothing, zilch, niente, it'll be healthy eating all round, till I get my personal slogan, and anyway how did this little nobody of a minister Zou Loukia come up with his 'I accuse' that everyone's talking about, eh, the Presidential Security Services tell me there are even babies being called 'I accuse,' and what about those young girls on heat getting it tattooed onto their backsides and the clients who, in an ironic twist, demand that the prostitutes have it, you'll appreciate, I think, what a colossal fuck-up this represents, it's not even as if it was rocket science to think up in the first place, a phrase like that, are the Minister for Agriculture's Negroes better than you, eh, do you realise, I wonder, that his Negroes don't even have an official car each, they get the ministry bus, they live off pitiful salaries, while you loll about here in the palace, swimming in my pool, drinking my champagne, sitting about watching foreign tv on cable, listening to their lies about me, eating my petit-fours, eating my salmon and my caviar, strolling about in my garden, taking your mistresses skiing on my artificial snow slopes, I'm surprised you don't sleep with my twenty wives, I start to wonder why I even have a cabinet, is that what I pay you for, to sit around here all day doing nothing, eh, why don't I just hire my own stupid dog as head of cabinet, tell me that, you bunch of good-for-nothings," and President Adrien Lokouta Eleki Mingi walked out slamming the door of the cabinet behind him, still shouting "you bunch of Negroes, things are going to change in this palace, I've had it with fattening up slavering slugs like you, let's start judging by results, to think some of you went to ENA and the *écoles polytechniques*, ENA my arse!"

the Negroes of the cabinet set about their arduous task with a Chaka Zulu spear and a sword of Damocles dangling over their heads while the palace walls still echoed with the president's final words, and around midnight, since they still hadn't thought of anything—there's plenty of petrol in this country, but not many ideas—it naturally occurred to them to phone a well known member of the Académie Française who was apparently the only black person in the history of this august assembly, and everyone applauded this last minute idea, and everyone said the academician in question would consider it a further honour, so they wrote him a long letter full of smoothly phrased imperfect subjunctives, and even some particularly moving passages composed in classical alexandrines with identical rhymes, they checked it carefully for punctuation, they didn't want to be sneered at by the academicians, who would take any opportunity to prove their use to the world, besides handing out the Top Prize for novels, and the president's Negroes almost came to blows over it, because some of them said there should be a semi-colon in place of a comma and others didn't agree and wanted to keep the comma to move the phrase up into fifth gear, and those in the latter camp stuck to their point even though it was contradicted by a certain Adolphe Thomas in the *Dictionary of Difficulties in the French Language*, whose view supported that of the first camp, and the second camp refused to yield and the point of all this was to get on the right side of the black academician who, as they were humbly aware, was one of the first ever Doctors of French Grammar from the African continent, and everything might have passed off smoothly if Adrien's Negroes hadn't then said that the academician would be slow to reply, the spear of Chaka Zulu and the sword of Damocles would come down on them before they received word from the Coupole, which is the name given to the onion dome beneath which these immortal sages sit listening to the distant babble of the French language and decree absolutely that such and such a text is the degree zero of all writing, but there was another reason why the Negroes beat a retreat, one member of the cabinet, who'd come top in his year at the ENA and owned the complete works of the black academician in question, pointed out that he had already produced a phrase for posterity, "reason is Greek, emotion is black," as an ENA graduate himself he explained to his colleagues that actually the academician couldn't come up with a second slogan because posterity isn't like the court of King Petaud where nobody's boss and anarchy rules, you only get one chance to coin a phrase, otherwise it's all just hollow chatter, much ado about nothing, that's why phrases that go down in History are short, sharp and to the point, and since such phrases survive through legends, centuries and millennia, people unfortunately forget who the true authors were, and fail to render to Caesar what is Caesar's

undaunted, the Negroes of the President and General of the armies came up with something else at the last minute, they decided to put all their ideas and everything they had found into a hat, they said it was called *brainstorming* in the smart colleges some of them had been to in the USA, and each of them wrote down on a piece of paper several phrases that had gone down in the history of this shitty world, and started to go through them, like they do in countries where you have the right to vote, reading each one out in a monotonous voice under the authority of the chief negro, beginning with Louis XIV, who said *"I am the State,"* and the leader of the Negroes of the President and General of the armies said "no, that quote's no good, we're not having that one, it's too self-regarding, it makes us sound like dictators, next!," Lenin said *"Communism is Soviet power plus the electrification of the entire country,"* and the chief black said "no, that's no good, it's disrespectful to the people, especially in a country where they can't even pay their electricity bill, next!," Danton said *"Boldness, and again Boldness, and always Boldness!,"* and the chief black said "no, no good, too repetitive, besides, people will think we're not bold enough, next!," Georges Clemenceau said *"War is too serious to be left to the generals,"* and the chief black said "no, no good, the military won't like that, we'll have a Coup d'État every five minutes with that one, the President himself is a general of the armies, don't forget, we need to watch our step, next!," Mac-Mahon said *"I am here. I shall remain here,"* and the chief black said "no, no good, sounds like a man unsure of his charisma clinging to power, next!," Bonaparte said, during the Egyptian campaign, *"Soldiers, from the height of these pyramids, forty centuries look down on you,"* and the chief black said "no, no good, it makes the soldiers sound uncultured, as though they've never read the works of the great historian Jean Tulard, it's our job to show people soldiers *aren't* idiots, next!," Talleyrand said *"This is the beginning of the end,"* and the chief black said, "no, no good, they'll think we mean the end of our regime, and we're meant to be in power for life, next!" Martin Luther King said *"I have a dream,"* which irritated the chief black, he hates any mention of MLK over Malcolm X, his idol, so he said "no, no good, we're fed up with utopias, everyone's always waiting for their own to come true, and I can tell you they'll be waiting a good few hundred years yet for that to happen, next!," Shakespeare said *"To be or not to be, that is the question,"* and the chief black said "no, no good, we've got past wondering whether we are or whether we aren't, we've already settled that one, we've been in power here for twenty three years, next!" and the President of Cameroon, Paul Biya, said *"Cameroon is Cameroon,"* and the chief black said "no, no good, everyone knows Cameroon will always be Cameroon, it's not as though any other country's going to even try to steal its identity or its Lions, who are, in any case, unbeatable, next!" the former Congolese President, Yombi Opangault, said *"A tough life today for a sweet life tomorrow,"* and the chief black said "no, no good, don't take the people of this country for fools, why not a sweet life today and to hell with tomorrow, hmm, besides the guy who said that lived in the most disgraceful luxury of all time, come on, next!" Karl Marx said *"Religion is the opium of the people,"* and the chief black said "no, absolutely not, we spend our whole time trying to persuade the people that our President and General of the armies is God's elect, and everyone will get steamed up about religion again, don't you know every single church in this country is subsidized by the president himself, come on then, next!" and President François Mitterrand said *"Time will take care of time,"* but the chief black got cross at this, you mustn't mention Mitterrand to him, and he said "no, no good, that guy took all the time in the world for himself, he spends his whole life riding roughshod over his friends and his enemies, then bows out to take up his seat at the right hand of God the father, no way, next!" Frédéric Dard alias San-Antonio said *"Fight your brother when he's shorn,"* and the chief black said "no, no good, too many bald people in this country, especially in the government, we mustn't rub them up the wrong way, I'm bald myself, next!," Cato the Elder said *"delenda Carthago,"* and the chief black said "no, no good, people in the south will think it's some phrase in northern patois and the people in the north will think it's a phrase in southern patois, best to avoid misunderstandings, on we go, next!" Pontius Pilate said *"Ecce homo,"* and the chief black said "no, no good, same applies as to Cato the Elder's flights of fancy, next!" as Jesus was dying on the cross he said *"My God, My God, why have You forsaken me?"* and the chief black said "no, no good, too pessimistic, too whiney, really, for a guy like Jesus, he could have really fucked things up here below with all the power he had, next!" Blaise Pascal said *"If Cleopatra's nose had been shorter it would have changed the face of the world,"* and the chief black said "no, no good, we're talking politics here, not plastic surgery, move on, next!" and so the president's Negroes looked through thousands of quotations and all sorts of other historic sayings and found nothing suitable for the country's most important citizen, because each time the chief black said "no, no good, move on, next!" and then at five in the morning, before the first cock crowed, one of the advisers who'd been flicking through some black and white documentaries at last hit upon a historic phrase

at exactly midday, just as the entire population sat down to a delicious meal of chicken-bicycle, the President and General of the armies took over the radio programmes and the only tv channel in the country, it was a solemn occasion, the president stretched taut as the skin of a bamileke drum, it was hard to choose exactly the right moment for leaving a phrase to posterity, and on that memorable Monday he was dressed in his Sunday best, wearing his heavy gold medals, looking from then on like a patriarch in the autumn of his reign, in fact he was so much dressed in his Sunday best, on that memorable Monday, you'd have thought it was the day of the Feast of the Goat, which we celebrate in memory of his grandmother, clearing his throat to overcome his nerves, he began by criticising the countries of Europe, who dazzled us with the sun of independence, when in fact we're still dependent on them, since we still have avenues named after General de Gaulle and General Leclerc and President Coti and President Pompidou, but in Europe there are no avenues named after Sese Soto, or Idi-Amin-Dada, or Jean-Bédel-Bokassa or any of the other fine men known personally to him, and valued for their loyalty, humanity and respect of the rights of man, in that sense we are still dependent—they take our oil but withhold their ideas, they cut down our forests to keep themselves warm in winter, they educate our leaders at ENA and the Polytechnique and turn them into little white Negroes, the Banania Negroes are back again, we thought they'd disappeared into the bush, but here they are, ready for action, thus spoke our president, his breath short, his fist punching the air, and this speech on the ills of colonialism led him on to a denunciation of the cruelty and challenges of capitalism, he said all that was utopia, and worst of all were the homegrown lackeys of the colonialists, the guys living in our country, who eat with us, dance in our bars, sit next to us on public transport, work in our fields, our offices, our markets, these double edged knives who do things with our wives which the memory of my mother who died in the river Tchinouka prohibits me mentioning, these men are actually moles of the imperial forces, and let's just say the President and General of the armies' anger shot up by ten notches at this point, because he hates those lackeys of imperialism and colonialism, as one might hate chigoes, bugs, fleas or worms, and the President and General of the armies said they must be tracked down, these criminals, these puppets, these hypocrites—"Tartuffes," he called them, "Malades Imaginaires," "Misanthropists," and "Paysans Parvenus," he said the proletariat revolution will triumph, the enemy will be crushed, driven back, wherever he may appear, he said God was with us, that our country was eternal, as he was himself, he called for national unity, the end of tribal warfare, he told us we were all descended from a single ancestor, and finally he came to "The *Credit Gone Away* Affair," which was dividing the country, he praised the Stubborn Snail's initiative, and promised to award him the Legion of Honour, and finished his speech with the words he was determined to leave to posterity—and we knew these were the words because he said them several times over, arms stretched wide as though clasping a sequoia, he said "I have understood you" and his phrase too became famous throughout the land, which is why, for a joke, we common folk often say that "the minister accuses, the president understands."

FATOU DIOME

· *Senegal* ·

✤

from THE BELLY OF THE ATLANTIC

1

HE RUNS, TACKLES, dribbles, strikes, falls, gets up again, carries on running. Faster! But the wind's changed: now the ball's heading straight for the crotch of Toldo, the Italian goalie. Oh God, do something! I'm not shouting, I'm begging you: if you're the Almighty, do something! Ah, back comes Maldini, his legs knitting up the turf.

In front of the TV, I leap off the sofa and give a violent kick. Ouch, the table! I wanted to run with the ball, help Maldini get it back, shadow him halfway down the pitch so he could bury it in the back of the opponent's net. But all my kick did was spill my cold tea onto the carpet. At this exact moment I imagine the Italians tensing up, stiff as the human fossils of Pompeii. I still don't know why they clench their buttocks when the ball nears the goal.

"Maldini! Oh yes, great defending from Maldini, who passes to his keeper! And Toldo kicks it away. What a talent, this Maldini! A truly great player. Still staying loyal to AC Milan. Over a hundred caps for Italy! Amazing. Cesare, his father, was a fine player too; the family definitely has talent!"

The commentator would have liked to make up a poem in praise of Maldini, but in the heat of the moment he could only utter a string of exclamations.

Why am I telling you all this? Because I adore football? Not that much. Why, then? Because I'm in love with Maldini? No way! I'm not that crazy. I'm not starstruck. I don't crane my neck gazing up at the sky. My grandma taught me early on how to pick up stars: all you have to do is place a basin of water in the middle of the yard at night and they'll be at your feet. Try it yourself, you only need a small dish in the corner of the garden to see twenty-two stars, Maldini among them, chasing round in circles on the grass like rats in a maze. So, since I'm not writing Maldini a love letter, why am I telling you all this? Simply because not all viruses land you in a hospital. Some just work inside us like they do in a computer program and cause breakdown.

It's 29 June 2000 and I'm watching the European Cup. It's Italy *v.* Holland in the semi-final. My eyes are staring at the TV, but my heart's contemplating other horizons.

Over there, people have been clinging to a scrap of land, the island of Niodior, for centuries. Stuck to the gum of the Atlantic like bits of leftover food, they wait resignedly for the next big wave that will either carry them off or leave them their lives. This thought hits me every time I retrace my path and my memory glimpses the minaret of the mosque, rigid in its certainties, and the coconut palms, shaking their hair in a nonchalant pagan dance whose origin is forgotten. Is it one of those ancient funeral dances that sanctifies the reunion of our dead with our ancestors? Or the oft-repeated one that celebrates marriages at the end of the harvest, after the rainy season? Or even that third kind of dance sparked by storms, during which, they say, the coconut palms imitate the shudder of young girls given in marriage to men they don't love? The fourth is the most mysterious, the dream tango, and everyone has their own version that follows the rhythm of their breathing.

It's nearly ten years since I left the shade of the coconut palms. Pounding the asphalt, my imprisoned feet recall their former liberty, the caress of warm sand, being nipped by crabs and the little thorn pricks that remind you there's life even in the body's forgotten extremities. I tread European ground, my feet sculpted and marked by African earth. One step after another, it's the same movement all humans make, all over the planet. Yet I know my western walk has nothing in common with the one that took me through the alleys, over the beaches, paths and fields of my native land. People walk everywhere, but never towards the same horizon. In Africa, I followed in destiny's wake, between chance and infinite hopefulness. In Europe, I walk down the long tunnel of efficiency that leads to well-defined goals. Here, chance plays no part; every step leads to an anticipated result and hope is measured by appetite for the fight. In the Technicolor world, you walk differently, towards an internalized destiny you set yourself regardless, without ever realising, for you're pressed into the modern mob, caught up in the social steamroller ready to crush all those who dare pull over onto the hard shoulder. So, under the grey European sky, or in unexpected sunlight, I walk on, counting my steps, each one bringing me closer to my dream. But how many kilometres, how many work-filled days and sleepless nights still separate me from that so-called success that my people, on the other hand, took for granted from the moment I told them I was leaving for France? I walk on, my steps weighed down by their dreams, my head filled with my own. I walk on and have no idea where I'll end up. I don't know which mast the flag of victory is hoisted on, nor which waters could wash away the stain of failure. Hey, you, don't nod off; my head's boiling over! Pass me the wood! This fire needs stoking. Writing's my witch's cauldron; at night I brew up dreams too tough to cook.

The noise of the television shakes me from my reverie. Every time the commentators shout Maldini's name, a face fills the screen. Thousands of kilometres from my sitting room, on the other side of the earth, in Senegal, on that island barely big enough to accommodate a stadium, I picture a young man glued to a battered old TV set, watching the same match as me. I feel him next to me. Our eyes meet on the same images. Hearts thudding, gasps, outbursts of joy or despair, all our emotions are synchronised while the match plays, because we're right behind the same man: Paolo Maldini.

So, over there, at the ends of the earth, I see a young man on a mat or an old bench stamping his feet in front of an ancient TV, which, despite its sputtering, commands as big an audience as a cinema screen. The owner of the only TV in the area generously sets it up in his yard and all the neighbours flock unannounced. The place is open to everyone; the sex, age and number of spectators vary according to the programme. This afternoon, 29 June 2000, the weather's good, the sky's a perfect blue and the TV isn't crackling, even if the owner had to bang it with his fist to get it going. The eyes trained on it have all the freshness of innocence. Boys in the flower of youth, their bodies formed by long years of running after balls made of rags, then unhoped-for footballs, jostle and press together, liquid energy streaming down their smooth foreheads. Alert to every move, they yell out their predictions.

One of the young men is silent, concentrated on the images. He leans towards the screen; his gaze weaves among the heads. Jaw clenched, only the odd jerky movement betrays the passion inside him. At Maldini's first tackle, his foot spontaneously strikes the bum of the boy squatting in front of him, hoofing him into the air. The victim turns round in a fury but, seeing the guilty party's face utterly engrossed, doesn't count on an apology and finds a place a little further off. You don't step on a blind man's balls twice, the saying goes: once is enough for him to pick up his merchandise as soon as he hears the sound of footsteps. The boy should shift his arse anyway, because the match was only just beginning and there'd be many more exciting moments. Already it's enough to make you commit hara-kiri: a red card for Zambrota, the Italian number 17. That's too much for the young man. As frustrated as Dino Zoff, the Italian coach, he straightens up and mutters something the ref wouldn't have liked. You get it: he supports the Italians and from now on you're not allowed to support any other team, out of respect. Fate really is against them: a yellow card for Francesco Toldo, the Italian keeper, who just grabbed hold of the Dutch number 9. The young man stands up, clutching his head in his hands, waiting for the inevitable punishment which soon follows: penalty against Italy.

Do something, God! Should I stop shouting? No, but you've no idea! It's not important? Of course it's important! Yes, I know, it's not Hiroshima. If that was all, I couldn't care less, but don't you see they might score a goal that will break Madické's heart! Who's Madické? Who's Madické? You think I've got time to tell you that? A penalty's not a coffee break; it rips out as fast as a footballer's fart! So are you going to do something or what? What about all my prayers, what about Ramadan? You think I do all that for nothing?

Toldo, the Italian goalie, saves it. Madické gives a violent kick, but this time no one's in the way. Phew! We've avoided the worst. His chest heaves with a long sigh, he relaxes, and his face lights up with a smile I know won't last. The match goes on.

Every time the Italians make a mistake, he puts his hands together in prayer. Just before half-time, Maldini argues with the ref's decision and is rewarded with a yellow card. Madické's smile's wiped off his face; he knows a second yellow card is the same as a red and his idol will be sent off. He squeezes his head in his hands with worry: he doesn't want to see his hero relegated to the sidelines. He'd like to talk to him, tell him the tactics he's devising, right there on his bench. Short of playing alongside him, he'd like to lend Maldini his legs, so he'd have a spare pair. But there, on that bench, his feet burrowing in the white, burning sand, how many dream kilometres separate him from the traces of mud Maldini will leave in the dressing rooms at half-time?

Transforming his despair into dialogue, he screams words that catch in the tops of the Niodior palms, never to reach Maldini's ears. I'm his devoted messenger: Madické and I have the same mother. People who only love by halves will tell you he's my half-brother, but to me he's my little brother and that's that.

So tell Maldini his yellow or red cards are too much to bear, they're crushing my heart. Tell him to save his skin, stay in one piece, not land a ball in the face, not let the opposition mow him down. Tell him I groan every time he cops it. Tell him his hot breath is searing my lungs. Tell him I feel his injuries and bear the scars. Tell him above all that I saw him, in Niodior, chasing the bubble of a dream over the warm sand. Because one day, on waste ground, my brother turned into Maldini. So tell Maldini about his wrestler's body, his dark eyes, his frizzy hair, his gorgeous smile and white teeth. That Maldini is my little brother, swallowed up in his dream.

The ref blows the half-time whistle, the young spectators make for the tree opposite the house, partly to stretch their legs but also to argue more loudly without disturbing their host. Only Madické stays by the house. He wouldn't miss the second half for the world. Nothing but ads on the TV now. Even in these regions, where drinking water's still a luxury, Coca-Cola brazenly comes to swell its sales figures. Have no fear, Coca-Cola will make the Sahel wheat grow! The TV attracts a group of scrawny seven- to ten-year-olds, their only playthings the sticks of wood and tins they've picked up in the street, who burst out laughing at the ad's suggestive scene: a boy approaches a group of girls who seem to be ignoring him. He offers a Coke to the prettiest one and beckons to her; the girl, after a refreshing gulp, generously offers him her waist. He puts his arm around her and they leave together, smiling. The boys guffaw. One asks another: "What's he going to do to her?"

The others snigger. The apparent leader of the gang answers, digging him with his elbow: "You stupid or what? He's going to screw her."

Encouraged by the leader, another boy goes on: "They're having a dance at the back of my house. I saw my big brother and his friends bring cases of Coca-Cola. Wahey! The girls are going to get what's coming to them!"

The laughter breaks out louder than ever. Now it's Miko's turn to whet their appetites. An enormous ice-cream cone, colours glistening, fills the screen, then a chubby little boy appears, greedily licking a huge ice cream. Envious purrs replace the inanity of a moment ago: a chorus of "Mmm! Oooh! That's good! Mmm!" These kids know ice cream only through images. For them it's a virtual food, eaten only *over there,* on the other side of the Atlantic, in the paradise where that plump kid had the good sense to be born. But they're crazy for that ice cream; for its sake they've memorised the advertising schedule. They chant the word "Miko," repeat it the way believers intone their holy book. They look forward to this ice cream as Muslims look forward to the paradise of Muhammad, and come here to await it like Christians awaiting the return of Christ. They've found icons for this Miko cone; they've made rough sculptures out of bits of wood, painted them with red and yellow crayons to represent mouthwatering ice creams. And it's these sticks of wood they sniff now as they savour the ad. I dream of a Miko swimming pool, built in the name of pleasure, not turnover. They dream of devouring this ice cream as Madické dreams of shaking Maldini's hand.

The ads draw to an end. The older boys, who were arguing about the match under the tree, gather in front of the television again and shoo away the younger boys, who are too noisy. Elders are respected around here. An old fisherman, still strong, dressed in rags, makes himself comfortable right in front of Madické, who identifies him by the smell of fish penetrating his nostrils. Greetings are polite but brief. That smell is fetid but respect shuts you up. Madické keeps quiet. He knows that in these parts the decades you've accumulated are aces that trump everything. He'll have to put up with this putrefying fossil for the whole of the second half. So he concentrates and imagines he's over there, where the match is being played, far from the old fisherman.

The stadium reappears. The players aren't out of the dressing rooms yet, but the commentators are warming up, and Maldini's name keeps being mentioned. What are they saying about him? Madické wonders. He strains to hear; it's not easy with his neighbours commentating the match like seasoned experts. He leans in nearer to the flickering screen, cups his ear in his hand as if better to isolate himself from the group, and listens again. The commentators' voices are slightly more audible, but the language they use flies past his ears without really going in. It's so annoying! And that smell, too, getting stronger and stronger . . . Only Maldini's name reaches him clearly at odd intervals. But what the hell are they saying about him?

And yet he's often heard, even seen, that language. Yes, he's seen it, here in his country: that language wears trousers, suits, ties, shoes with laces; or skirts, suits, sunglasses and high heels. He does recognise the language that flows in Senegalese offices, but he doesn't understand it and that irritates him. The second half begins.

The first free kick goes to the Italians. Madické's delighted. They've pulled themselves together, he thinks, and that reassures him. But his optimism's soon frustrated. The Dutch value their honour. They defend their goal like a nun defends her fanny. The Italians have to deal with it. This sublimated war on the turf demands nerves of steel, and it's not easy holding out for ninety minutes. Especially in these last moments of the match when every move counts. Madické sweats; it's hot, and, besides, that stink of fish is beginning to turn his stomach.

The ref whistles an end to the ninety minutes; the adversaries will have to wait for extra time to fight on. Although their thirst for glory keeps them on their feet, their ravaged faces beg for rest. Like a protective mother, a sister moved to tears or a devoted wife, I'd like to offer them a drink, sponge their faces, bandage their cuts and give them a hug. I'd like to tell them their frustrating match is like life: the best goals are always yet to come; it's just that waiting for them is painful.

Covered in mud and streaming with sweat, the players huddle together, their shoulders slumped, crushed by so much fruitless effort.

Rest before extra time. The group of young spectators who've stayed in front of the television becomes animated. The match is upsetting their forecasts. The nervous ones are keen to assert their point of view, waving their hands about. The advertising jingles ring out. The kids from before rush over. The old fisherman picks a quarrel to kill time; with a teasing smile, he taps Madické on the shoulder and, stroking his beard, says: "What's happening? Maldini, eh? Eh? Not up to it today, huh? Your opponents are looking pretty solid."

Madické looks up at the man before fixing his eyes on the dusk-filled horizon. There's something disarming in silence, in knowledge, too. The old man's feeling inspired and won't back down. Coming over all learned, he keeps preening his beard and utters a deep thought that's just occurred to him: "You know, Maldini, the greater the obstacle you overcome, the more dazzling your success. The quality of the victory depends on the merit of the opposition. Beating a coward doesn't make a man a hero."

This rambling is hardly a consolation to Madické. He's heard this Neanderthal philosophy before—this exotic verbiage, falsified a thousand times, dumped on us by westerners, the better to sideline us. Enough already with all these convenient proverbs. Didn't the old fisherman know, conversely, that losing to a brave adversary doesn't make a man a hero either?

The sun seemed to flee human questioning and threatened to plunge into the Atlantic. The sky, fired up with passion, looked lower than usual, leaving a hanging trail of reddish light over the tops of the coconut palms. The sea breeze, in its mercy, brushed the skin almost imperceptibly. Only a few women on their way back from the well, late with their domestic chores, noticed the dusk's light wind, which swept under their cotton *pagnes* to caress them where the sun never sees. It was devoted women such as these, too, who dared disturb the village's incipient calm with the last pounding of their pestles. Thump! Thump! Thump! These pestles, distant and repetitive, reverberated in the depths of Madické's heart. Because he'd heard them all his life, he recognised them, could even decode them: they always precede the call of the muezzin and the owl's song. For all the islanders they've become the music that heralds the night. But in this superstitious universe, they also mark the hour of the evil spirits and the moment ancestral fears slip into the shadows.

When, as a kid, he'd hear the pounding of the pestles, Madické would leave the improvised playgrounds, following his friends, and run back to our mother. He knew exactly where to find her: she was always in her kitchen at this hour, at the far end of the back yard, busy cooking supper or grinding a fistful of millet to make the milk curd porridge for the next day. If by some unhappy chance she wasn't there, he'd take his little bench and settle down in the kitchen in front of the fire, to avoid his dread of the creeping shadows outside. Impatiently, he'd stave off his boredom by feeding wood to the fire, marveling at the dancing flames until a voice, feigning severity, reached his ears.

"Hey, stop that, Madické! What a blaze you're making! You'll burn my supper!"

Time had passed. The uneasy atmosphere of dusk still drove him to seek the reassurance of skirts, but no longer his mother's. In any case, on this 29 June 2000 the most beguiling of nymphs couldn't have held his gaze.

The magical curtain of ads is torn. The younger boys scatter, echoing the last notes of their favourite song: Miko! Miko! Sunk in black, the yard looks like a marine graveyard. Only the bluish glow from the old television weakly illuminates the spectators' faces. The silence is proper for contemplation. The muezzin yells himself hoarse for nothing. He'll just have to have some mint tea afterwards; it'll do him good! The stadium reappears, the faithful cheer their gods. The old fisherman noisily clears his throat, shakes his neighbour's arm and announces, as if confiding in him: "Maldini, my son, the moment of truth is upon us."

Madické gives the requisite faint smile before taking his arm back, irritated by a foul by Jaap Stam, a Dutch player.

"Red card!" he yells.

But the ref's satisfied with a yellow.

"Shit, he should've got a red card! That ref's a right b—"

The sentence is left unfinished; no one knows where anger will end. The Dutch are undeterred. They're more and more audacious. Aron Winter makes his point forcefully and wins a corner. Eighty-four caps earns you a lot of experience, especially in cheating. Seedorf fancies himself to take the corner. Delvecchio rushes forward, proving to his mum that her milk wasn't wasted: she definitely suckled a hero, capable of restoring hope to the entire Italian nation. But the Dutch mothers have done the same, and their sons, eager to make them proud, go back on the attack. Cannavaro blocks and gets it away; Maldini sprints off. Madické peels off his bench, imagining he's right behind him: "Come on! Go for it! You can do it! Go!" he shouts, practically rupturing his vocal cords.

Everything you want, you've got it!

A cousin who'd been deported from the USA never stopped listening to that song and translated it for anyone who wanted to hear: where there's a will there's a way. Madické's beginning to have his doubts, and justifiably so.

The two periods of extra time remain goalless. Now a penalty shootout's inevitable. Madické knows this, and his heart's beating wildly in his breast. He presses his hand to it but that doesn't help; the palpitations increase.

The mistress of the house calls everyone for supper. The meal here isn't reserved for those who live in the house; everyone who's around when it's served is welcome and automatically invited to share it. A young girl brings a small calabash filled with water for everyone in turn to wash their hands, while her mother places a series of steaming bowls in the middle of the yard. The fisherman briefly rinses his paws and makes a beeline for the head of the family. Discussing how bad the catch has been lately, he positions himself cross-legged on a mat and begins to pay tribute to the woman's efforts. Mmm! You can smell the spices in the *talalé*, a dish fit for a king! Our women are the only ones who can make such delicious fish couscous, and that's a fact!

As for Madické, his stomach's in knots. A late lunch is his excuse to decline the invitation politely. Besides, unlike the older generation, he doesn't like sharing other people's meals whenever circumstances dictate. If this match hadn't gone on, he'd have extricated himself before supper-time. While some wolf down mouthfuls of couscous and compliment the cook to justify their greed, he savours the calm created in front of the TV.

"Great," he says to himself, "I can watch the penalties in peace."

But the weather decided otherwise. He'd hardly had this thought when a series of lightning flashes ripped through the sky. A violent tornado whipped the coconut palm branches. The white sand, the islanders' pride, became their worst enemy, a whirlwind flagellating their skin and carrying off everything in its path. The people eating quickly deserted their mats, which were either flung against the fence or swirled above their heads. Then big raindrops began to fall: one of the first June rains, often short-lived but always unpredictable, that let Sahelians know it's the start of the winter season and time to work in the fields.

Madické hadn't waited for the first drops of water to seize the old set and carry it into the living room, but in vain. At the first flash of lightning, the TV had blinked and then, letting out a last beep, had abruptly died. He didn't want to think the worst: that beep wasn't a last sigh; the TV couldn't have given up the ghost. He told himself it was an electrical whim, just a shock, a kind of heart attack brought on by the virulence of the lightning flashes. In the living room he attempted a long, solitary resuscitation, with no success. He needed to hear the owner's verdict to convince him to leave the patient's bedside: "I think it's dead. There's nothing you can do; it doesn't like the rainy season. Last year, too, it died on me at the first clap of thunder. Luckily I managed to get it going again. This time, I think it's finished."

With his hand resting on the television, the man smiled as he talked on. Glancing at the living room clock, Madické realised bitterly that the penalty shoot-out was finished, too. He politely stammered some excuses and left.

BOUBACAR BORIS DIOP

· *Senegal* ·

❖

from MURAMBI, THE BOOK OF BONES

Translated by Fiona McLaughlin

Jessica

"THEY LOVE EACH other like crazy, those two. And now events are forcing them to postpone the date of their marriage again!"

"Ah! Lucienne and her boyfriend Valence Ndimbati . . . It's so sad," I say distractedly.

You get used to anything very fast. In her hometown of Nyamata, where my friend Mukandori is looking for a refuge, we find a way to chatter on like two old women. She asks me suddenly, stopping:

"Do you really think they're going to do it?"

I've learned a lie.

"It's impossible, Theresa. They're looking mainly to scare people. It'll calm down in a few days."

The idea that from now on she could be killed at any moment by anybody seemed very odd to her.

As for me, I lead a double life. There are things that I can't talk about to anyone. Not even to Theresa.

For example, this message dated April 8, 1994, that I've just received from Bisesero. Stéphanie Nkubito, our comrade in that district, wrote it a few hours before being discovered and slaughtered. It seems to me that they didn't take the time to question him. They suspected that he was a member of the Rwandan Patriotic Front, operating in Bisesero. The letter from our comrade shows just how organized and determined the killers are. They're really ready to go all out this time around.

Stéphanie tells me that on Thursday, April 7, 1994, Abel Mujawamarya, a businessman from Kigali, arrived in Gisovu with the two yellow trucks full of machetes. He had them unloaded at the home of Olivier Bishirandora. The latter, who has a forge in his workshop, immediately started sharpening the machetes. Olivier, a member of Parmehutu/DRM, was also the mayor of Gisovu in the seventies, during the time of President Kayibanda.

Abel Mujawamarya then organized a meeting, during which he gave out machetes and grenades to the Hutus. The Interahamwe then started to terrorize the Tutsis, accusing them of having murdered their beloved president, Juvénal Habyarimana. They set to, looting and setting fire to the Tutsis' houses, and then killed some of them. The Tutsis started fleeing their houses to take refuge in the parish churches of Mubaga and Kibingo, as well as in the Mugonero hospital. Others preferred to head for the mountains.

Stéphanie Nkubito asks me to make a note and spread the word that the inhabitants of Bisesero, those tough warriors, intend to put up a fight. Since 1959, every time there are massacres, they get organized and at least succeed in driving back their attackers. At times they've even been able to get back their stolen animals through bold punitive expeditions. That's why, adds Stéphanie, their reputation for being invincible is circulating around Rwanda. Refugees are flocking in from all over the place. But between the lines of his letter, Stéphanie's fears were clear: according to his sources, the government is intending to put an end to the myth of invincibility of the Abasero, as the Tutsis of Bisesero are called. The army will do the bulk of the work, and Interahamwe militia reinforcements will be dispatched from Gisenyi and other towns where, because of the relatively small number of Tutsis among their populations, the massacres will be over earlier than elsewhere.

I read and reread Stéphanie's message. At the bottom of the page there's a little drawing with the following caption: "Jessica Kamanzi making the victory sign."

Jessica Kamanzi, that's me. I smile as I look at my two fingers raised triumphantly toward the sky. Oh yes, victory is certain. I've never doubted it, not even for a moment. But it will be so bitter . . .

I'd love to keep the drawing as a memento of Stéphanie Nkubito. I finally decide to give it up: my comrade thinks he's being watched. I tear the message into pieces.

Theresa touches my arm:

"This is it," she says in a low voice.

We're in the neighborhood of the parish church of Nyamata, right near the lodgings of the Salesian Fathers, who people say are originally from Brazil. Behind the thick curtain of eucalyptus and acacia, we can see people hurrying by the hundreds into the church.

"I'm going," says Theresa. "You'd better come with me, Jessica."

I think the exact opposite. The fighters I came with into Kigali found out that future victims were being encouraged to take refuge in churches so that they could be exterminated there. But I have nothing else to propose to Theresa.

"Good luck," I say, averting my eyes from hers.

We were supposed to go to Lucienne's wedding the following Saturday, and she had thick and magnificent braids on her head.

"Jessie, they'll never be able to do anything, knowing that God can see them."

I hug her to me without replying.

On the way back everything is all right.

The weather is mild in Kigali. The streets are deserted and suddenly look wider. I realize that without noticing—and probably like every one of us—I had certain reference points in the city. A little shop at the street corner. Motorcycle repairers in the vicinity of a Perowanda gas station. Little things like that. Since the news of the assassination broke, all these tableaux have disappeared from the scene. The occasional people who dare leave their house are foreigners or, of course, Hutus. Or those IDs say they are. That's my case. The others are all hiding wherever they can.

In the city there's an excitement that's both joyful and solemn. Groups of Interahamwe militia in white outfits covered with banana leaves walk around singing. Standing in their tanks, the military and the police are keeping an eye on everything. Everyone has a transistor radio glued to his ear. The radio says: "My friends, they have dared to kill our good president Habyarimana. The hour of truth is at hand!" Then there're some music and games. The host of the program, in brilliant form, quizzes his listeners: "How do you recognize an Inyenzi?" The listeners call in. Some of the answers are really funny, so we have a good laugh. Everyone gives a description. The host becomes serious again, almost severe: "Have fun, my friends, but don't forget the work that's waiting for you!"

At Camp Kigali ten Belgian UN soldiers have been killed. Belgium is pulling out. They don't want to know anything else. Even their civilians are feeling threatened and they try to pass for French at the barricades. Somewhere in Paris some sinister civil servants are rubbing their hands together: the situation is under control in Kigali, the RPF won't get in. Their straw men got the army generals and commanders together. They uttered the terrible words: *Muhere iruhande*. Literally, "Begin with one side." Neighborhood by neighborhood. House by house. Don't spread your forces out in disorderly killings. All of them must die. Lists had been drawn up. The prime minister. Agathe Uwilingiyimana, and hundreds of other moderate Hutu politicians have already fallen to the bullets of the presidential guard. To tell what they did to Agathe Uwilingiyimana is beyond me. A woman's body profaned. After so-called *Ibyitso,* the collaborators, it'll be the Tutsis' turn. What they're guilty of is just being themselves: they're barred from innocence for all eternity.

If only by the way people are walking, you can see that tension is mounting by the minute. I can feel it almost physically. Everyone is running or at least hurrying about. I meet more and more passersby who seem to be walking around in circles. There seems to be another light in their eyes. I think of the fathers who have to face the anguished eyes of their children and who can't tell them anything. For them, the country has become an immense trap in the space of a few hours. Death is on the prowl. They can't even dream of defending themselves. Everything has been meticulously prepared for a long time: the administration, the army, the Interahamwe are going to combine forces to kill, if possible, every last one of them.

I've chosen to be here. The resistance leaders at Mulindi placed their trust in me and I accepted. They explained to us that the Arusha peace treaty could produce either the best or the worst of results and that the RFP needed people in all the big cities and towns.

On the eve of our departure I thought a lot about my father. In my brothers and sisters' opinion I was his favorite. Even he didn't attempt to hide it. When we were in Bujumbura sometimes he would say, "Of all my children, Jessica is the one who is most like me." A funny character, Jonas Sibomana. He would show us his torso, furrowed with scars, and would promise to leave all his goods to the one of us who could reproduce the same scars on his own body. My brother Georges, who didn't take anything seriously, answered him, "You're so broke, old Jonas, that it's not even worth it to try." Then both of them would pretend to fight and we had so much fun watching them run all over the house. My father had been a member of Pierre Mulele's resistance movement in Kwilu. Oh, he wasn't one of the important people in the group. He was just one of those peasants they give weapons to, explaining to them quickly who the enemies are. They could lose their lives in all that, but they wouldn't make a name for themselves. Jonas told me that he saw Che Guevara when the Cuban came to organize the resistance in the Congo. He also knew Kabila, and didn't have a good word to say about him. When he felt very ill, in Bujumbura, he called for me: "Go to the house where we used to live in the neighborhood of Buyenzi, and tell the owner that it's your father, Jonas Sibomana, who sent you. He'll understand." The owner and I found a big package in a hole next to a spigot. I opened it. It contained three old guns, already half rusted. When I went back to see him we had a good laugh at his joke.

I suppose that's what made me decide to interrupt my studies when I was eighteen to join the guerrillas in Mulindi.

I remember everything as if it were yesterday. There were fifteen of us young people making the road trip by night from Bujumbura to the Mushiha refugee camp. Departure the next day already, at dusk—because we always had to move about in the dark—for Mwanza in Tanzania where we had to wait for the boat—the *Victoria*—for a week. After that, it was Bukoba. There we were supposed to locate a red truck parked at the port. The leader of our group, Patrick Nagera—he was to fall later in the front line of our October 1990 offensive—started looking all around him, his nose in the air. A large man in a hat, with a scarf around his neck, passed close to him and said very quickly without stopping, "Is it you?" Later on it was in Mutukura and Kampala where we stopped seeing each other. I was staying with a family in the Natete neighborhood. In the evening, when I took a stroll in the street to stretch my legs a bit, I was puzzled to see cars driving on the left-hand side of the road. It's strange, but that's my strongest memory of Natete, cars driving on the wrong side. All I had to do was to wait for the signal for my departure. I had understood that I was not to ask questions of my hosts.

If we were recounting all this today, one might think that I was bragging. That's not the case. Ever since 1959, every young Rwandan, at one moment or another in his life, has to answer the same question: Should we just sit back and wait for the killers, or try to do something so that our country can go back to being normal? Between our futures and ourselves, unknown people had planted a sort of giant machete. Try as you might, you couldn't ignore it. The tragedy would always end up catching you. Because people came to your house one night and massacred all your family. Because in the country where you live in exile, you always end up feeling in the way. Besides, what could I, Jessica Kamanzi, possibly brag about? Others have given their lives for the success of our struggle. I have never held a gun nor participated in the military actions of the guerrillas. I stayed almost the whole time at Mulindi to take care of the cultural activities of the resistance. Sure, I was at Arusha during the negotiations. I typed or photocopied documents and sometimes I was called on to give summaries to our delegates. But those were only humble tasks. It's true that my presence in Kigali today is not without danger. It's maybe the first time that I've risked my life. In this country, where all the citizens are watched night and day, my false ID card probably won't protect me for very long. I have to move all the time. But sooner or later there'll be someone who'll ask me some very precise questions that I'll have a hard time answering.

While I'm walking I think back on our night watches. We used to sing, "If three fall in combat, the two who are left will free Rwanda." Very simple words. We didn't have time for poetic tricks. These words come back to me like an echo and give me strength. The moment of liberation is at hand. Since this morning our units have been moving on

Kigali. But will they arrive everywhere in time? Unfortunately, no. In certain places, the butchery has already started.

Near Kyovu I see hundreds of corpses a few yards from the barricade. While his colleagues are slitting the throats of their victims or hacking them to bits with machetes close to the barricade, an Interahamwe militiaman is checking ID cards. The visor of his helmet is turned backwards, a cigarette dangles from his mouth, and he is sweating profusely. He asks to see my papers. As I take them out of my bag he doesn't take his eyes off me. The slightest sign of panic, and I'm done for. I manage to keep my composure. All around me there are screams coming from everywhere. In these first hours of massacre the Interahamwe surprise me with the assiduity and even a certain discipline. They are really set on giving the best of themselves, if it is possible to speak this way of the bloody brutes. A woman they've wounded but are waiting to finish off a bit later comes toward me, the right part of her jaw and chest covered with blood. She swears that she's not a Tutsi and begs me to explain to the man in charge of the barrier. I move away from her very quickly. She insists. I tell her dryly to leave me alone. Seeing this, the Interahamwe militiaman is convinced that I'm on his side. He blurts out in a joyful peal of laughter:

"Ah! You're hard-hearted, my sister, so you are! Come on, you should take pity on her!"

Then he brutally pushes the woman back toward the throat slitters before checking the ID cards again.

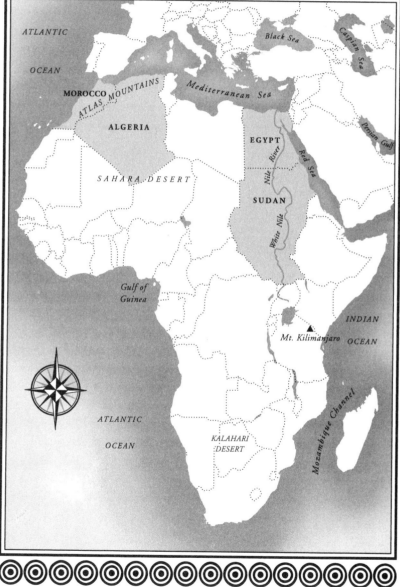

ATLANTIC

OCEAN

MOROCCO

ATLAS MOUNTAINS

ALGERIA

SAHARA DESERT

Black Sea

Caspian Sea

Mediterranean Sea

EGYPT

Nile River

Red Sea

Persian Gulf

SUDAN

White Nile

Gulf of
Guinea

INDIAN

Mt. Kilimanjaro

OCEAN

ATLANTIC

OCEAN

KALAHARI
DESERT

Mozambique Channel